taste.
LOW FAT

Over 100 mouth-watering recipes

igloo

igloo

Published in 2010
by Igloo Books Ltd
Cottage Farm
Sywell
NN6 0BJ

www.igloo-books.com

10 9 8 7 6 5 4 3 2 1
ISBN: 978 1 84852 841 3

Food photography and recipe development: Stockfood, The Food Image Agency

Printed and manufactured in China.

contents.

introduction.

So why pursue a low-fat diet? Obviously it is one of the most popular means of losing weight, but it is also an excellent way of ensuring good health and preventing disease… if done in moderation! Many people mistakenly see any fat as to be avoided at all costs. However, many of the diverse types of fat in our food are not just good for us, but are necessary for our bodies to function properly.

Most people nowadays are familiar with the terms describing the main types of edible fats: saturated fats (usually solid at room temperature and found in greatest quantities in animal products such as meat, poultry and dairy produce); polyunsaturated fats (generally liquid at room temperature and derived from vegetables and nuts); and monounsaturated fats (again, generally liquid and richest in nuts, seeds and other vegetable sources, like olives and avocados). It is important, though, to realize that most foods contain a mixture of all three types in varying proportions.

All fats are necessary as they help carry the fat-soluble vitamins A, D and E around the body and provide us with energy. Too much saturated fat, though, can upset the body's way of dealing with cholesterol, resulting in high levels of it in the blood and eventually furring of the arteries and possible heart disease. Cholesterol is, in fact, yet another type of fat, which the healthy body needs, produces for itself when necessary and keeps at a steady level unless there is too much saturated fat in the diet.

On the other hand, the two unsaturated types of fats can have really positive effects. Monounsaturates, like those predominant in olive oil, are known to reduce the level of 'bad' (sticky) cholesterol in the blood and increase levels of 'good' cholesterol, which helps remove the 'bad' stuff. Polyunsaturates also lower 'bad' cholesterol but have the added advantage of including the Essential Fatty Acids (EFAs), needed by the body and which it cannot produce itself. Perhaps the best-known of these are the omega fats, like omega-3, which can help ward off all sort of ailments, such as heart disease, arthritis and cancers.

So the strong message when cutting down fat in your diet is to cut down most strongly on saturates, leaving room for the good and necessary fats. So favour oily fish (packed with essential omega 3s) over red meats, seek out low-fat dairy products like milk, yoghurt and cheeses instead of full-fat versions (either those marketed as 'low-fat' or those, like the curd cheese quark, that are naturally very low in fat); use olive and sunflower oils in cooking instead of hard fats. You can even reduce the fat content of salads by replacing some or all of the oil in the dressing with lemon juice or low-fat yoghurt.

This is not to say that you can't eat your favourite foods. Enjoy red meat once in a while, but make sure it is well trimmed of visible fat and try to skim away any liquid fat produced in cooking. Make meat stews, pasta sauces, etc., the day ahead, let them get cold, then spoon away the fat congealed on top before reheating to serve. Cook chicken and duck in their skins for maximum flavour, but remove these before serving, as most of the fat in poultry lies in the skin. Make use of turkey more than just once a year, as it naturally very low in fat and considered a 'superfood' by many as it is rich in important nutrients. Game birds and venison are also low in fat and full of goodness. In desserts, use low-fat Greek-style yoghurts in place of cream and make sorbets rather than ice creams.

If you are trying to reduce the amount of fats in your diet, beware the huge amount of hidden fats in processed foodstuffs such as cakes, biscuits, fast foods and margarines. It is not just that they can contain unexpectedly large amounts of fat, it is that these tend to be what are known as 'partially hydrogenated fats', made from vegetable oils treated to be solid at room temperature. Also often termed 'trans fats', they have no nutritional benefit and are particularly effective at raising levels of 'bad' cholesterol.

The wide and exciting range of recipes that follow are carefully designed with all this mind. Arranged in chapters on Starters, Light Bites, Dips & Tapas, Soups & Stews, Main Meals, Salads and Desserts, they offer readers the ability to prepare interesting and satisfyingly healthy low-fat food for any type of occasion, from family meals to special celebrations and dinner parties.

starters.

Prawn cocktail with mango

Prep and cook time: 30 minutes
Cannot be frozen
Serves: 4

Ingredients:

1 large ripe mango, peeled and cubed
1 small red bell pepper, seeds removed, cut into strips
1 bunch rocket|arugula, roughly chopped
1 handful bean sprouts
12 prepared king prawns
2 garlic cloves, roughly chopped
4 tbsp olive oil
1 untreated orange
3 tbsp balsamic vinegar

Nutritional information:
kcal: 496.07
fat: 20.6 g
saturated fat: 2.6 g

Method:

Mix the mango, bell pepper, rocket/arugula and bean sprouts together.

Lightly fry the prawns and garlic together in 1 tbsp oil.

Grate the orange zest and then juice the orange. Add both to the prawns, remove from the heat and allow to rest.

Mix the balsamic vinegar with the rest of the oil, salt and pepper and mix in with the salad ingredients. Season to taste and serve in bowls with the prawns on top.

Aubergine towers with tomato salsa and mozzarella

Prep and cook time: 45 minutes
Cannot be frozen
Serves: 4

Ingredients:
2 aubergines|eggplants, cut into 12 slices
4 tbsp olive oil
1 clove garlic, finely chopped
1 shallot, finely chopped
3 tomatoes, seeds removed and diced
3 tomatoes sliced very finely
1 tbsp parsley, chopped
2 balls mozzarella (150 g | 6 oz each)

To garnish:
4 sprigs parsley

Nutritional information:
kcal: 369.5
fat: 20.3 g
saturated fat: 6.5 g

Method:

Heat the oven to 200°C (180°C fan) 400°F, gas 6.

Arrange the aubergines/eggplants on a grill pan and season with salt and ground black pepper. Take 2 tbsp olive oil and use to brush over the aubergines.

Grill for 5 minutes, turn and cook for 5 more minutes until golden.

Meanwhile, heat the rest of the oil and fry the garlic and shallot for 2 minutes. Add the diced tomatoes, season with salt and pepper and simmer for 2 minutes. Then add the parsley.

Drain the mozzarella and cut into 12 slices.

Take 8 aubergine/eggplant slices and top each one with a tomato slice, season with salt and pepper and a mozzarella slice.

Layer up two together and lay the remaining aubergine/eggplant slice on top. Pour some of the tomato salsa over the tower and top with another slice of mozzarella.

Bake in the preheated oven for 5 minutes until the cheese begins to melt.

Serve with the remaining tomato salsa and garnish with parsley.

Fish cakes with lime, chilli and coriander

Prep time: 40 minutes
Cannot be frozen
Serves: 4

Ingredients:
450 g | 16 oz | 3 cups potatoes
450 g | 16 oz cod fillet, chopped
2 tbsp fish sauce
6 spring onions | scallions, chopped
pinch of Cayenne pepper
300 g | 11 oz | 7/8 cup prepared prawns | shrimps
3 tbsp vegetable oil

To garnish:
1 small red bell pepper, cut into thin strips
2 limes, quartered
8 sprigs coriander | cilantro
4 tbsp sweet chilli sauce

Nutritional information:
kcal: 465.6
fat: 23.05 g
saturated fat: 2.9 g

Method:
Boil the potatoes for 30 minutes in salted water. Drain, then mash.

Mix the fish, fish sauce, spring onions/scallions and some Cayenne pepper in with the potatoes.

Add the prawns and season with salt.

Shape into 8 fish cakes.

Heat the oil and fry the fish cakes for 5 minutes on each side until golden brown.

Garnish with the bell pepper strips, lime quarters and coriander/cilantro leaves. Serve with sweet chilli sauce.

Meaty courgette parcels

Prep and cook time: 45 minutes
Cannot be frozen
Serves: 4

Ingredients:

2 courgettes|zucchinis, cut into long thin slices
3 tbsp olive oil
1 onion, finely chopped
1 carrot, finely chopped
200 g | 7 oz ground meat
1 egg yolk
2 tbsp bread crumbs
50 g | 2 oz | 1/2 cup Parmesan cheese, finely grated
1 tbsp basil, finely chopped

Nutritional information:
kcal: 349.7
fat: 22.7 g
saturated fat: 7.6 g

Method:

Finely dice the ends of the courgettes/zucchinis that you haven't used to make the thin slices.

Heat the oil in a skillet and fry the onion in 1 tbsp oil until transparent.

Add the carrot and the diced courgette/zucchini and gently fry for 1–2 minutes.

Remove from the heat and let cool slightly. Mix together in a bowl with the meat, egg yolk, bread crumbs, Parmesan and basil. The mixture should be easy to shape. Season with salt and ground black pepper.

Lay two courgette/zucchini slices in a cross one over the other. Place the filling in the middle, fold over the courgette/zucchini slices and hold in place with a wooden toothpick. Continue until all slices are used up.

Fry the parcels in 2 tbsp oil for 5–6 minutes.

Lentil burgers with a yoghurt dip

Prep and cook time: 1 hour 30 minutes
Cannot be frozen
Serves: 4

Ingredients:
200 g | 7 oz | 1 cup brown lentils
1 sprig thyme
1 bay leaf
1 stale wholewheat roll
1 onion, finely chopped
2 garlic cloves, finely chopped
3 tbsp sunflower oil
5 tbsp parsley, finely chopped
1 chilli pepper, seeds removed, finely chopped
1 carrot, grated
2 tbsp sesame seeds
1 pinch ground cumin
1 pinch ground coriander
1 pinch nutmeg
1 pinch Cayenne pepper
1 egg
2 tbsp spelt flour
2 spring onions|scallions, cut into rings
200 g | 7 oz | 3/4 cup low-fat yoghurt
3 tbsp wine vinegar
3 tbsp olive oil
1 pinch sugar
200 g | 7 oz mixed leaf salad, finely torn
100 g | 3 1/2 oz cherry tomatoes, halved
1 cucumber, sliced lengthways with a peeler

Nutritional information:
kcal: 461.5
fat: 15.03 g
saturated fat: 2.9 g

Method:
Heat the oven to 220°C (200°C fan) 425°F, gas 7.

Rinse the lentils under running water. Cook in a pan with a lid with 475ml / 2 cups water, the thyme sprig and the bay leaf for 35 minutes or until soft.

Remove the lid and heat vigorously stirring continuously until the liquid has evaporated and the lentils begin to disintegrate. Remove the thyme and the bay leaf.

Soften the bread roll in warm water, squeeze out excess water, roughly chop and add to the lentil mixture.

Fry the onion and garlic in 1 tbsp oil. Add to the lentils with the parsley.

Stir in the chilli, carrots, sesame, coriander, nutmeg and cumin. Season with salt and ground black pepper.

Add the egg and spelt flour to the mass and squeeze everything together.

Shape into 8 burgers and put onto a tray.

Brush the burgers with the remaining oil and cook for 12 minutes until golden brown.

To make the yoghurt dip, mix the spring onions/scallions with the yoghurt and season with salt.

To make the salad, mix the vinegar, oil, sugar and salt.

Arrange the salad on plates and drizzle over the dressing. Add 2 lentil burgers per plate and serve with the dip.

Cream cheese and carrot dumplings with a creamy leek sauce

Prep and cook time: 1 hour
Can be frozen
Serves: 4

Ingredients:

For the sauce:

1 leek
1 tsp sunflower oil
1 garlic clove, crushed
100 ml | 3 $^1/_2$ fl oz | $^2/_5$ cups sweet white wine
100 ml | 3 $^1/_2$ fl oz | $^2/_5$ cups vegetable stock
200 g | 7 oz | $^7/_8$ cup low-fat cream cheese
100 ml | 3 $^1/_2$ fl oz | $^2/_5$ cups milk

For the dumplings:

750 g | 26 oz 3 $^1/_4$ cups low-fat cream cheese
3 eggs
4 tbsp light cream, 15% fat
2 carrots, finely grated
200 g | 7 oz 1 | $^5/_8$ cups flour
150 g | 5 oz | 3 $^1/_3$ cups bread crumbs
nutmeg

To garnish:

parsley

Nutritional information:

kcal: 707.2
fat: 18.1 g
saturated fat: 5.9 g

Method:

Cut the leek in half lengthways and then cut the green part into very fine sticks 6–8 cm long. Cut the rest into rings.

Heat the oil and fry the leek rings with the garlic. Add the wine and the stock and reduce for 5 minutes. Add the cream cheese and simmer until the cheese has fully dissolved.

Add the milk and if necessary reduce further. Season the sauce with salt and ground pepper and keep warm on the lowest heat setting.

To make the dumplings drain the cream cheese and mix together with the eggs and the light cream to form a smooth paste.

Add the carrots, flour and bread crumbs and season with salt, pepper and nutmeg.

Shape 12 dumplings out of the dough and place them into a pot of simmering salt water. Turn the temperature down and cook for 15 minutes at a low heat. Do not allow to boil.

Remove the dumplings from the water using a draining spoon.

Arrange them on preheated plates with the cream sauce.

Sprinkle with the green part of the leek and parsley to garnish.

Duck spring rolls

Prep and cook time: 40 minutes
Cannot be frozen
Serves: 4 (20 spring rolls)

Ingredients:
20 rice paper sheets
2 carrots, sliced and cut into sticks
50 g | 2 oz | 1 2/3 cups glass noodles, raw
10 lettuce leaves
200 g | 7 oz smoked duck breast, skin removed, cut into thin strips 4–5 cm long
20 g | 3/4 oz | 3/4 cup fresh parsley
1 yellow bell pepper, seeds removed, cut into thin sticks 4–5 cm long
1/2 cucumber, seeds removed, cut into thin sticks 4–5 cm long
4 tbsp sweet chilli sauce

Nutritional information:
kcal: 309.4
fat: 4.5 g
saturated fat: 1.2 g

Method:

Dip the rice paper sheets one after the other in a bowl of lukewarm water until they soften. Remove and lay on kitchen paper and cover with a damp tea towel.

Blanch the carrot sticks in boiling salted water for 1 minute. Remove and drain.

Soften the glass noodles in boiling salted water, drain and dry well.

Lay 2 rice paper sheets on top of one another and lay a lettuce leaf on top. Place the carrots, duck, parsley, bell pepper, glass noodles and cucumber in the middle.

Fold the rice paper ends inwards and roll up. Cut each roll in half and arrange with the cut end upwards.

Serve with sweet chilli sauce or soy sauce for dipping.

Vegetable terrine with tomatoes, aubergines and courgettes

Prep and cook time: 1 hour 10 minutes
Cannot be frozen
Serves: 4 (1 terrine)

Ingredients:
1 red bell pepper, seeds removed, cut into strips
1 courgette|zucchini, finely chopped
1 aubergine|eggplant, finely chopped
2 beefsteak tomatoes, seeds removed, finely chopped
1 garlic clove, finely chopped
60 g | 2 oz | 1/2 cup flour
200 ml | 7 fl oz | 4/5 cups semi-skimmed milk
nutmeg
4 eggs, separated

To garnish:
basil

Nutritional information:
kcal: 229.3
fat: 9.3 g
saturated fat: 2.7 g

Method:

Heat the oven to 200°C (180°C fan) 400°F, gas 6

Put the bell pepper, courgette/zucchini and the aubergine/eggplant into a pan of boiling salted water and cook for 4 minutes until al dente.

Drain, refresh with cold water, then let dry on kitchen paper. Return to the dry pan and mix in the tomatoes, garlic and 1 tbsp flour.

Turn the vegetables into a greased and lined 900g / 2 lb loaf tin.

Mix the remaining flour with the milk, egg yolks and nutmeg until smooth.

Whisk the egg whites until softly peaking.

Fold the egg whites into the egg yolk mixture. Pour this mixture into the tin with the vegetables.

Half fill a roasting tin with water. Sit the vegetable terrine in the centre.

Cook for 35–45 minutes until firm.

Cool then remove the terrine from the tin and cut into slices.

Garnish with basil.

Grilled prawns with a tomato and cucumber salad

Prep and cook time: 45 minutes
Cannot be frozen
Serves: 4

Ingredients:
12 king prawns, heads removed, gutted and peeled up to the tail
12 kebab sticks
2 cloves garlic, crushed
2 tbsp olive oil
1 tbsp lemon juice

For the salad:
2 tbsp olive oil
4 tbsp white balsamic vinegar
4 tomatoes, halved and finely chopped
1 cucumber, peeled, cored and finely chopped
20 g | ⅓ cup parsley leaves

To garnish:
1 lemon, cut into 8 wedges

Nutritional information:
kcal: 241.4
fat: 12.3 g
saturated fat: 1.8 g

Method:

Skewer the prawns lengthways onto the kebab sticks.

Mix the garlic cloves with the oil and lemon juice and brush the prawns with the mixture. Marinate for 30 minutes.

To make the salad dressing, mix the oil, balsamic vinegar, salt and pepper. Mix together the tomatoes, cucumber and parsley and add the dressing. Season and divide into four bowls.

Grill the prawns on all sides for 2–3 minutes on a hot grill. Serve with the salad and lemon slices.

Potato cakes with feta and tomatoes

Prep and cook time: 1 hour
Can be frozen
Serves: 4

Ingredients:
600 g | 21 oz | 4 cups potatoes, roughly chopped
1 onion, finely chopped
125 ml | 4 $^1/_2$ fl oz | $^1/_2$ cup milk
1 bay leaf
1 egg
200 g | 7 oz | 1 cup tomatoes, quartered, seeds removed and finely chopped
100 g | 3 $^1/_2$ oz | $^2/_3$ cup feta, crumbled
50 - 60 g | 2 - 2 oz | $^1/_2$ cup flour
2 tsp fresh thyme leaves, chopped oil, for frying

To garnish:
lettuce leaves
thyme leaves

Nutritional information:
kcal: 271.2
fat: 10.2 g
saturated fat: 4.5 g

Method:

Place the potatoes, onion, milk and the bay leaf in a pot. Add 1 tsp salt and cook for 25 minutes with a lid on.

Remove the bay leaf and mash the potatoes.

Add the egg, tomatoes and feta to the mashed potatoes and stir in enough flour until the mixture becomes firm enough to shape. Mix in the thyme and season with salt and pepper.

Shape the dough into 8 rounds, then flatten.

Heat a non-stick skillet and brush with oil. Fry the potato cakes for 2–3 minutes on each side until golden brown.

Keep the finished potato cakes warm in the oven (80°C / 175°F / low). Serve with lettuce.

Marinated chicken kebabs with a nectarine salsa

Prep and cook time: 45 minutes Marinating: 2 hours
Cannot be frozen
Serves: 4

Ingredients:
For the kebabs:
1 chilli pepper, roughly chopped
1 shallot, finely chopped
2 garlic cloves, sliced
1/4 tsp ground cumin
1/4 tsp ground coriander
2 tbsp light soy sauce
4 tbsp coconut milk
1 tbsp sesame oil
4 chicken breasts, 120 g | 4 oz each, cut into thin strips

For the nectarine salsa:
1 tsp sesame oil
1 shallot, finely chopped
1 garlic clove, finely chopped
3 nectarines, peeled and finely chopped
1 red bell pepper, finely chopped
1 pinch ground ginger
pinch of Cayenne pepper
1 - 2 tbsp apple vinegar
2 tbsp fresh basil, chopped

Nutritional information:
kcal: 275.2
fat: 6.7 g
saturated fat: 1.1 g

Method:

Mix the chilli, shallot, garlic, cumin, coriander, soy sauce, coconut milk and the sesame oil.

Add the chicken strips, cover, chill and marinate for 2 hours.

Heat the sesame oil in a skillet and fry the shallot and garlic until transparent. Add the nectarines and bell pepper and fry for 2-3 minutes. Season with ginger, salt, ground black pepper, Cayenne pepper and vinegar.

Remove from the heat and allow the flavours to mingle 30 minutes.

Thread the chicken onto kebab sticks in a wave-like motion.

Grill for 8 minutes, brushing with the marinade and turning occasionally.

Just before serving, add the basil to the nectarine salsa and season well with salt and ground black pepper.

Serve the chicken with the nectarine salsa.

soups & stews.

Tomato and red pepper soup with croutons

Prep and cook time: 45 minutes
Can be frozen
Serves: 4

Ingredients:
1 onion, finely chopped
1 garlic clove, finely chopped
1 tbsp tomato puree
2 tbsp olive oil
2 red bell pepper, seeds removed, finely chopped
250 g | 9 oz | 1 cup canned tomatoes
500 ml | 18 fl oz | 2 cups vegetable stock
150 ml | 5 fl oz | ⅔ cups vegetable juice
1 bay leaf
1 pinch sugar
2 tbsp low-fat crème fraiche

For the croutons:
2 slices bread, crusts removed, diced
1 tbsp olive oil
1 tbsp fresh parsley

To garnish:
4 sprigs parsley

Nutritional information:
kcal: 152.8
fat: 10.4 g
saturated fat: 1.6 g

Method:

Sauté the onion and garlic with the tomato puree in olive oil. Add the bell pepper and simmer for 5 minutes.

Add the tomatoes, stock and juice and bring to a boil. Season with salt, ground black pepper and the bay leaf and simmer, covered on a low heat for 20 minutes.

Turn off the heat and use a hand blender to whizz to a smooth soup. Add the sugar.

To make the croutons, fry the bread in hot oil for 2 minutes until golden brown. Add the parsley and dry on kitchen paper.

Pour the soup into hot bowls and add a dollop of crème fraiche.

Garnish with croutons and parsley.

Potato stew with onions and basil

Prep and cook time: 15 minutes Cooking: 20 minutes
Cannot be frozen
Serves: 4

Ingredients:
2 tbsp olive oil
4 red onions, sliced
1 kg | 35 oz | 5 3/4 cups baking potatoes, cut into chunks
1 bay leaf
400 ml | 14 fl oz | 1 2/3 cups vegetable stock
2 tbsp fresh basil, chopped

Nutritional information:
kcal: 261.1
fat: 7.2 g
saturated fat: 1.1 g

Method:

Heat the oil in a pot and fry the onions and potatoes for a couple of minutes. Season with salt and ground black pepper and add the bay leaf.

Pour in the stock and simmer covered for 20 minutes.

Serve sprinkled with basil.

Cold courgette and avocado soup

Prep and cook time: 25 minutes Chilling: 1 hour
Can be frozen
Serves: 4

Ingredients:
500 ml | 18 fl oz | 2 cups vegetable stock
4 small courgettes|zucchinis, finely chopped
2 ripe avocados
juice of 1 lime
200 ml | 7 fl oz | 4/5 cups natural yoghurt
3 mint leaves
50 g | 2 oz bunch watercress
pinch ground cumin
lime slices, to garnish

Nutritional information:
kcal: 181.2
fat: 16.7 g
saturated fat: 2.5 g

Method:
Bring the stock to a boil and add the courgettes/zucchinis. Allow to simmer for 4–5 minutes until soft.

Remove from the heat, let cool and then chill for about 1 hour.

Halve, peel and finely chop 1 1/2 avocados and drizzle immediately with lime juice so it doesn't go black.

Add to the courgette/zucchini soup along with the yoghurt, mint and watercress.

Season with a pinch of cumin, a pinch of salt, and ground black pepper; puree using a hand blender until creamy. If necessary re-season.

Divide the courgette and avocado soup into 4 bowls. Chill for 1 hour.

Chop reserved avocado and use to garnish along with the lime slices.

Cold tomato and shrimp soup

Prep and cook time: 25 minutes Cooling: 1 hour
Can be frozen
Serves: 4

Ingredients:

1 cucumber, finely chopped
500 g | 18 oz | 3 cups ripe tomatoes, chopped
1 red bell pepper, halved, seeds removed and finely chopped
1 yellow bell pepper, halved, seeds removed and finely chopped
1 clove garlic, crushed
200 ml | 7 fl oz | 4/5 cups vegetable stock
3 tbsp balsamic vinegar
2 sprig basil, finely chopped
2 tbsp olive oil

To garnish:

2 shallots, halved lengthways and sliced
2 tbsp olive oil
8 prepared prawns|shrimps
24 basil leaves

Nutritional information:

kcal: 157
fat: 9.5 g
saturated fat: 1.4 g

Method:

Put the cucumber, tomatoes, red and yellow bell peppers and garlic together into a blender or food processor.

Pour in the vegetable stock and blend to a smooth soup consistency. Add a little more stock for a more runny consistency, if you like.

Push through a metal sieve into a jug and season with salt and ground black pepper, then add the vinegar.

Add the basil and the oil into the soup and let it cool for at least an hour.

To serve, fry the shallots in 1 tbsp oil for a few minutes, then add the shrimps and cook for 1 minute. Season with salt and ground black pepper.

Serve the chilled soup in cold bowls, garnished with prawns/shrimps, shallots and basil leaves.

Cold cucumber soup with smoked salmon and sour cream

Prep and cook time: 30 minutes
Cannot be frozen
Serves: 4

Ingredients:

2 small cucumbers, chopped
1 garlic clove, chopped
2 spring onions|scallions, finely chopped
250 ml | 9 fl oz | 1 cup still mineral water
1 tsp Dijon mustard
3 - 4 tbsp lemon juice
1 tsp sugar
½ tsp cumin
3 tbsp dill, roughly chopped

To garnish:

40 g | 1 ½ oz smoked salmon, cut into strips
4 tsp sour cream
4 sprigs of dill

Nutritional information:

kcal: 62.4
fat: 0.7 g
saturated fat: 0.6 g

Method:

Place the cucumber, garlic, spring onions/scallions and cucumber into a blender and puree until smooth.

Add the mineral water, adding more if necessary, until the soup reaches a smooth pouring consistency.

Add the mustard, lemon juice, salt, ground black pepper, sugar and cumin.

Add the dill into the soup. Leave to cool for one hour.

Before serving, season once more with salt and pepper. Serve in bowls or on deep plates each with a tsp of sour cream.

Twirl the salmon strips in the middle and garnish with dill and some ground black pepper.

Minestrone alle erbe

Prep and cook time: 35 minutes
Cannot be frozen
Serves: 4

Ingredients:

3 tbsp olive oil
1 onion, finely chopped
2 garlic cloves, finely chopped
250 g | 9 oz | 1 1/3 cups tomatoes, seeds removed and finely chopped
150 g | 5 oz fresh | 1 1/3 cups green|string beans, halved
1 tsp fresh rosemary, chopped
800 ml | 28 fl oz | 3 1/2 cups vegetable stock
150 g | 5 oz 1 1/5 cups elbow macaroni
150 g | 5 oz white 1 1/3 cups broad|fava beans
1 courgette|zucchini, cut in half lengthways and diagonally sliced
2 tbsp balsamic vinegar

To garnish:
rosemary leaves
basil leaves

Nutritional information:
kcal: 218.3
fat: 12.3 g
saturated fat: 1.4 g

Method:

Heat the oil in a pot and sauté the onions and the garlic. Add the tomatoes and the green/string beans and fry lightly for a few minutes.

Add the rosemary, stock and the macaroni and cook gently for 6 minutes or until the pasta is almost done.

Add the broad/fava beans and the courgette/zucchini. Season with salt, pepper and balsamic vinegar and cook for 4 more minutes until macaroni and vegetables are tender

Serve, garnished with rosemary and basil leaves.

Miso soup with tofu

Prep and cook time: 10 minutes Cooking: 10 minutes
Cannot be frozen
Serves: 4

Ingredients:
2 tbsp oil
2 garlic cloves, finely chopped
1 bunch spring onions|scallions, cut into rings
2 tsp fresh ginger, grated
1 large cucumber, seeds removed, finely chopped
1000 ml | 35 fl oz | 4 cups vegetable stock
4 tbsp light miso paste
3 - 4 tbsp light soy sauce
300 g | 11 oz | 1 cup tofu, diced
3 - 4 tbsp coriander|cilantro leaves, finely chopped
pinch Cayenne pepper
2 tbsp lemon juice

Nutritional information:
kcal: 241.3
fat: 16.1 g
saturated fat: 1.9 g

Method:
Heat the oil and fry the garlic, spring onions/scallions and ginger. Add the cucumber then add the stock, miso paste and soy sauce. Simmer for 4–5 minutes.

Add the tofu and the coriander/cilantro and season with Cayenne pepper and lemon juice. Re-heat, pour into bowls and serve.

Provencal-style vegetable stew

Prep and cook time: 40 minutes
Cannot be frozen
Serves: 4

Ingredients:

4 tbsp / 1/4 cup olive oil
2 aubergines|eggplants, trimmed and sliced
1 red bell pepper, seeds removed and cut into thick strips
1 yellow bell pepper, seeds removed and cut into thick strips
3 courgettes|zucchinis, trimmed and sliced
2 onions, peeled and quartered
100 ml | 3 1/2 fl oz | 2/5 cups dry white wine
1 sprig fresh rosemary, needles removed
2 garlic cloves, peeled and sliced
400 g | 14 oz can chopped tomatoes

To garnish:
rosemary sprigs

Nutritional information:
kcal: 185.3
fat: 11.1 g
saturated fat: 1.7 g

Method:

Heat half the oil in 2 large skillets. Add the aubergines/eggplants to one and the onions to the other.

Fry for a 5 minutes, to soften, then add the courgettes/zucchinis to the aubergines/eggplants and the peppers to the onions and cook for 5 more minutes.

Combine all the vegetables in 1 large skillet and splash in the wine. Cover and simmer for 10 minutes.

Add the rosemary, garlic and tomatoes.

Simmer for a further 10 minutes until the vegetables are tender.

Season with salt and ground black pepper.

Garnish with fresh rosemary sprigs.

Chickpea and tomato stew with meatballs

Prep and cook time: 50 minutes
Can be frozen
Serves: 4

Ingredients:

200 g | 7 oz chorizo sausage
1 onion, finely chopped
1 tbsp olive oil
1 yellow bell pepper, halved, seeds removed, chopped
1 red bell pepper, halved, seeds removed, finely chopped
400 g | 14 oz | 1 1/4 cups canned tomatoes
400 ml | 14 fl oz | 1 2/3 cups vegetable stock
150 g | 5 oz | 3/4 cup chickpeas|garbanzo beans, drained from can
1 tbsp fresh sage leaves, chopped

To garnish:

20 small sage leaves

Nutritional information:

kcal: 364.4
fat: 22 g
saturated fat: 6.5 g

Method:

Squeeze the chorizo out of its skin and form into small balls.

Carefully fry the meatballs in hot oil together with the onion for 3 minutes.

Tip out the fat, dry the pan with absorbent paper and return the meatballs and onion to the pan.

Add the peppers and fry for 2 minutes.

Add the tomatoes, the stock and the drained chickpeas/ garbanzo beans and simmer for 10–15 minutes stirring occasionally.

Season with salt and ground black pepper and add the sage.

Pour into warm bowls and garnish with sage.

Lentil and carrot soup

Prep and cook time: 25 minutes
Cannot be frozen
Serves: 4

1 tbsp olive oil
400 g | 14 oz | 3 1/4 cups carrots, sliced
6 spring onions|scallions, cut into rings
1 garlic clove, finely chopped
800 ml | 28 fl oz | 3 1/2 cups vegetable stock
125 g | 4 1/2 oz | 2/3 cup red lentils
100 g | 3 1/2 oz | 1/2 cup natural yoghurt
2 tbsp crème fraiche
2 tbsp mixed herbs (chervil, parsley, chives), chopped

To garnish:
4 sprigs parsley

Nutritional information:
kcal: 230.9
fat: 9.3 g
saturated fat: 2.4 g

Method:

Heat the oil and add the carrot, spring onions/scallions and fry for a few minutes.

Pour on the stock. Add the lentils and simmer 10 minutes. Season with salt and ground black pepper and pour into bowls.

Mix the yoghurt, crème fraiche and the herbs and pour onto the soup.

Garnish with parsley to serve.

Vegetable stew with cabbage and chickpeas

Prep and cook time: 1 hour 5 minutes
Can be frozen
Serves: 4

Ingredients:

2 tbsp olive oil
2 shallots, finely chopped
2 garlic cloves, finely chopped
1 small savoy cabbage, stem removed and shredded
1 tbsp tomato puree
600 ml | 21 fl oz | 2 1/2 cups vegetable stock
200 g | 7 oz | 1 cup chickpeas|garbanzo beans, drained from can
2 tomatoes, finely chopped
1 tsp fresh root ginger, grated
1 chilli pepper, halved, seeds removed and finely chopped
50 g | 2 oz | 1/2 cup Parmesan cheese, roughly grated

Nutritional information:
kcal: 247.3
fat: 16.1 g
saturated fat: 4.1 g

Method:

Heat the oil in a skillet and fry the shallots and the garlic for a couple of minutes, to soften.

Add the cabbage and fry gently for about 2 minutes.

Stir in the tomato puree and the stock.

Add the chickpeas/garbanzo beans, tomatoes, ginger and chilli pepper and simmer, covered, for 45 minutes, stirring occasionally.

Season with salt and ground black pepper and serve with grated Parmesan.

main

courses.

Steamed fish fillet with coriander leaves

Prep and cook time: 20 minutes Steam: 12 minutes
Cannot be frozen
Serves: 4

Ingredients:
800 g | 28 oz white fish fillet, cut into four equal pieces
3 carrots, cut into thin sticks
200 g | 7 oz | 1 1/4 cups celeriac|celery root, cut into thin sticks
1 small leek, cut into thin sticks
150 ml | 5 fl oz | 2/3 cups white wine
100 ml | 3 1/2 fl oz | 2/5 cups vegetable stock

To garnish:
4 coriander|cilantro leaves

Nutritional information:
kcal: 230.2
fat: 1.8 g
saturated fat: 0.3 g

Method:
Season the fish with salt and ground black pepper.

Put the fish into a steamer and top with the carrots, celeriac/celery root and leek.

Pour the wine and the stock into a pot and bring to the boil.

Place the steamer over the pot, cover and steam for 10–12 minutes until the fish and vegetables are tender.

Arrange on plates and garnish with coriander/cilantro leaves. Serve with soy sauce.

Salmon with mango salsa and rice

Prep and cook time: 45 minutes
Cannot be frozen
Serves: 4

Ingredients:
For the salsa:
1 mango, peeled, flesh removed from stone and finely chopped
1 red onion, finely chopped
1 apple, finely chopped
1 lime, juiced and zest finely grated
2 tbsp sweet chilli sauce

For the rice:
175 g | 6 oz | 1 cup long grain rice
1 clove garlic, crushed
1 bell pepper, seeds removed and finely chopped
4 spring onions|scallions, chopped

For the salmon:
1 tbsp olive oil
4 salmon fillets

Nutritional information:
kcal: 441.2
fat: 13.4 g
saturated fat: 3 g

Method:
Put the mango, onion, apple, lime zest and juice, and the sweet chilli sauce together in a bowl. Stir to mix. Cover and allow the flavours to mingle whilst preparing the rest of the dish.

Put the rice into a pan with 2 cups of water, a generous pinch of salt, the garlic, the bell pepper and the spring onions/scallions. Cover and simmer for 15 minutes until the rice is tender and the liquid absorbed.

Brush the olive oil over the salmon fillets and season with salt and ground black pepper.

Fry in a non-stick skillet for 10 minutes, turning as needed.

Spoon the rice onto plates, top with the salmon fillets and some mango salsa.

Sea bass fillet with leeks and cherry tomatoes

Prep and cook time: 35 minutes
Cannot be frozen
Serves: 4

Ingredients:

3 leeks, sliced
400 g | 14 oz | 2 1/5 cups cherry tomatoes
225 ml | 8 fl oz | 1 cup fish stock
3 tbsp dry white wine
4 pieces sea bass fillet, 150 g each
2 tbsp lemon juice
2 tbsp olive oil

Nutritional information:
kcal: 294.3
fat: 11.4 g
saturated fat: 1.5 g

Method:

Heat the oven to 200°C (180°C fan) 400°F, gas 6.

Place the leeks and tomatoes in a baking dish and add the stock and the wine. Season with salt and pepper and place the fish fillets on top.

Drizzle the fish fillets with lemon juice and season with salt and ground black pepper.

Pour over the olive oil and cover with tin foil.

Bake in the preheated oven for 20 minutes, or until the fish and vegetables are tender.

Cod loin with ginger served on pepper and bean sprouts

Prep and cook time: 30 minutes
Cannot be frozen
Serves: 4

Ingredients:
150 ml | 5 fl oz | ⅔ cups dry white wine
1 piece root ginger (20 g), finely sliced
600 g | 21 oz cod loin, cut into four equal pieces
1 tbsp peanut oil
2 red bell peppers, cut into strips
200 g | 7 oz | 2 cups bean sprouts
2 tbsp soy sauce
pinch of Cayenne pepper

Nutritional information:
kcal: 215.4
fat: 5.4 g
saturated fat: 0.7 g

Method:
In a large skillet bring the white wine and the ginger to a boil. Add the fish. Cook for around 15 minutes at a low heat with a lid on.

Heat the oil in a skillet or a wok. Fry the pepper for 3 minutes stirring continuously. Add the bean sprouts and leave to cook for around 2 minutes.

Season with soy sauce and Cayenne pepper and serve on plates. Arrange the fish on top of the vegetables and drizzle with the ginger broth.

BBQ sea bass with kaffir lime and bay leaves

Prep and cook time: 30 minutes
Cannot be frozen
Serves: 4

Ingredients:
2 prepared sea bass
8 fresh kaffir lime leaves, cut in half lengthways
8 fresh bay leaves, cut in half lengthways
2 - 3 tbsp olive oil, for brushing

To garnish:
1 lemon, quartered
several bay leaves

Nutritional information:
kcal: 219.1
fat: 7.8 g
saturated fat: 1.3 g

Method:
Using a sharp knife, gently cut into the fish making 8 diagonal cuts on each side. Place the kaffir lime leaves and bay leaves into the cuts.

Brush the fish with oil, season with salt and ground black pepper and place on the BBQ or in a grill pan.

Grill slowly at a low heat for 8–10 minutes on each side, turning occasionally.

Serve with lemon slices.

Beef fillets with pears poached in red wine

Prep and cook time: 35 minutes
Cannot be frozen
Serves: 4

Ingredients:
2 tbsp oil
1 shallot, peeled and finely chopped
250 ml | 9 fl oz | 1 cup dry red wine
1 tbsp balsamic vinegar
4 pears, peeled, halved and pitted
half a cinnamon stick
1 tbsp cranberry sauce
4 x 160g | 5-6 oz beef fillet steaks

To garnish:
parsley

Nutritional information:
kcal: 348.5
fat: 17.8 g
saturated fat: 3.4 g

Method:

Heat the oven to 200°C (180°C fan) 400°F, gas 6.

Heat 1 tbsp of oil in a pan and add the shallot and fry gently for 5 minutes to soften.

Add the red wine and balsamic vinegar, then add the pears and cinnamon. Simmer for 5 - 10 minutes so that the pears are just softened.

Remove the pears from the pan and continue simmering the liquid until reduced by half.

Season the beef fillets with salt and ground black pepper and fry on all sides to brown.

Cook in the oven for about 5 minutes until rare.

Remove the cinnamon from the wine mixture and stir in the cranberry sauce. Season with salt and pepper and put the pears back in.

Take the meat out of the oven and cut into thick pieces. Serve on plates with the meat arranged on top of the pears and the sauce. Garnish with parsley.

Saltimbocca (Italian veal escalope with sage)

Prep and cook time: 35 minutes
Cannot be frozen
Serves: 4

Ingredients:
8 thin slices rosé veal, 80 g | 3 oz each
8 slices Parma ham
8 sage leaves
2 tbsp olive oil
125 ml | 4 ½ fl oz | ½ cups
Marsala wine
sage leaves, to garnish

For the vegetables:
2 carrots, sliced
2 courgettes|zucchinis, sliced

Nutritional information:
kcal: 373.1
fat: 15.3 g
saturated fat: 6.2 g

Method:
Carefully tenderize the meat using the smooth side of a meat mallet.

Place 1 slice of Parma ham and 1 sage leaf on each slice of meat (if necessary hold in place with a wooden toothpick).

Heat the olive oil in a skillet. Add the escalopes and fry for 2 minutes on each side. Season with salt and ground black pepper.

Pour in the Marsala wine and bring to a boil, simmer to reduce slightly.

Blanch the carrots and courgettes/zucchinis in salted water for 2–3 minutes.

Serve the veal with the vegetables and drizzle with sauce.

Garnish with sage leaves.

Lamb kebabs with endives and olives

Prep and cook time: 40 minutes
Cannot be frozen
Serves: 4

Ingredients:

600 g | 21 oz lamb loin (prepared and trimmed), cut into 1 cm thick slices
8 sprigs rosemary
2 tbsp olive oil
2 red onions, cut into strips
2 garlic cloves, sliced
60 g | 2 oz black olives, stones removed and roughly chopped
3 tbsp balsamic vinegar
4 endives|chicory, halved, stalks removed
1 tbsp olive oil
1 tsp brown sugar
150 ml | 5 fl oz | 2/3 cups vegetable stock

To garnish:
oregano flowers

Nutritional information:
kcal: 433.7
fat: 27.1 g
saturated fat: 4.9 g

Method:

Skewer the meat onto the rosemary sprigs.

Brush 1 tbsp olive oil over the kebabs from all sides. Season with salt and ground black pepper and grill for 20 minutes, turning as needed.

Heat 1 tbsp olive oil in a skillet and fry the onion and the garlic for a few minutes, to soften. Add the olives.

Pour on the balsamic vinegar and 2 tbsp water and remove from the heat.

Heat 1 tbsp olive oil in a large skillet, add the endive/chicory and sprinkle over with the sugar. Season with salt and ground black pepper and pour on the stock.

Cook for about 10 minutes, turning occasionally, until the liquid has almost completely evaporated.

Arrange the lamb kebabs with the olive broth and the endive/chicory vegetables onto plates and serve garnished with oregano flowers.

Steak with roast potatoes, green beans and bacon

Prep and cook time: 50 minutes
Cannot be frozen
Serves: 4

Ingredients:

8 new potatoes (500 g | 3 cups), quartered lengthways
4 tbsp olive oil
500 g | 18 oz | 3 1/3 cups green|string beans
50 g | 2 oz | 1/5 cup bacon, diced
3 garlic cloves, roughly chopped
2 spring onions|scallions, just the white part, halved
4 fillet steaks, 140 g each

Nutritional information:
kcal: 462
fat: 24.6 g
saturated fat: 5.9 g

Method:

Heat the oven to 200°C (180°C in a fan oven) 400°F, gas 6.

Mix the potatoes with 2 tbsp olive oil. Season with salt and pepper and lay on a roasting tin. Roast in the oven for 15 minutes turning occasionally, until golden brown.

Blanch the beans in boiling salt water for 8 minutes. Drain and set aside.

Fry the bacon in a skillet. Add the garlic and the beans and season with salt and pepper and keep warm.

Add the spring onions/scallions to the potatoes and cook for 10 more minutes.

Fry the steaks in the remaining oil on both sides for 2-3 minutes. Season well with salt and ground black pepper, set aside and allow to rest.

Slice the steaks and arrange on plates with the beans, spring onions/scallions and potatoes.

Veal with courgette, tomatoes and mozzarella

Prep and cook time: 45 minutes
Cannot be frozen
Serves: 4

Ingredients:

500 g | 18 oz rosé veal fillet, cut into four equal pieces
30 g | 1 oz | 1 ¼ cups basil
4 tbsp olive oil
2 tbsp Parmesan cheese, freshly grated
1 courgette|zucchini, halved lengthways and cut into diagonal slices
2 ripe beefsteak tomatoes, sliced
250 g | 9 oz mozzarella, sliced
pinch of Cayenne pepper

Nutritional information:

kcal: 374.3
fat: 24.4 g
saturated fat: 8.8 g

Method:

Heat the oven to 200°C (180°C fan) 400°F, gas 6.

Gently tenderize the meat with a meat hammer.

Set aside a few basil leaves for the garnish and puree the rest with 3 tbsp olive oil. Mix in the Parmesan. Put the pesto mix to one side.

Place the courgette/zucchini slices in the bottom of an oven-proof dish and drizzle with 1 tbsp olive oil. Season with salt and ground black pepper.

Season the meat with salt and ground black pepper and lay on top of the courgette/zucchini. Place the tomato slices and mozzarella on top, season with some Cayenne pepper and bake in the preheated oven for 20–25 minutes.

Garnish with basil leaves and drizzle with the basil pesto.

Spicy pork fillet with shiitake mushrooms and rice noodles

Prep and cook time: 25 minutes Marinate: 30 minutes
Cannot be frozen
Serves: 4

Ingredients:
300 g | 11 oz 1/4 cup wide rice noodles
1 chilli pepper, finely chopped
3 tbsp sesame oil
500 g | 18 oz pork fillet, cut into strips
2 garlic cloves, finely chopped
1 leek, cut into thin strips
150 g | 5 oz 2 cups shiitake mushrooms, sliced
50 g | 2 oz unsalted peanuts
2 tbsp fish sauce
2 tbsp dark soy sauce
1 tbsp brown sugar
10 g | 1/4 oz fresh Thai basil, roughly chopped

To garnish:
1 red chilli, seeds removed and finely sliced
1 spring onion|scallion, finely sliced

Nutritional information:
kcal: 549.7
fat: 16.8 g
saturated fat: 3.1 g

Method:

Put the chilli pepper into a shallow dish with 1 tbsp sesame oil.

Add the pork, stir, cover, chill and marinate for 30 minutes.

Cook the noodles according to the directions on the packet and drain.

Heat 2 tbsp sesame oil in a wok and stir fry the pork for a few minutes.

Add the garlic and leek and stir fry for another 5 minutes.

Add the mushrooms and peanuts and fry for a further 3–4 minutes. Add a splash of water, if needed.

Season with fish sauce, soy sauce and sugar.

Stir in the noodles and warm through, then stir in the basil.

Serve garnished with red chilli and spring onion/scallion.

Stir fried chicken with vegetables

Prep and cook time: 40 minutes
Can be frozen
Serves: 4

Ingredients:
2 tbsp peanut oil
600 g | 21 oz chicken breasts, cubed
10 g | ¼ oz root ginger, grated
2 cloves garlic, crushed
60 g | 2 oz spring onions|scallions, roughly chopped
150 g | 5 oz green|string beans, trimmed and halved
120 g | 4 oz green pepper, deseeded and sliced
80 g | 3 oz celery, chopped
150 ml | 5 fl oz | ⅔ cups chicken stock
2 tbsp sweet chilli sauce
2 tbsp light soy sauce
80 g | 3 oz mangetout
80 g | 3 oz frozen peas
1 green chilli, deseeded and chopped
1 tbsp finely chopped coriander|cilantro leaves

To garnish:
2 coriander|cilantro leaves

Nutritional information:
kcal: 360
fat: 12.1 g
saturated fat: 2.1 g

Method:
Heat the oil in a wok, add the chicken and fry for 2 minutes over a high heat.

Add the ginger and garlic, reduce the heat and fry for a further 2 minutes.

Add the spring onions/scallions, beans, peppers, celery, chicken stock, chilli sauce and soy sauce, cover and cook for 2-3 minutes more.

Add the mangetout, frozen peas and chilli and cook everything for 2-3 more minutes, shaking the wok now and again. Season with salt and ground black pepper. Add the chopped coriander/cilantro leaves.

Garnish with coriander/cilantro leaves and serve.

Spicy pork tagliatelle

Prep and cook time: 50 minutes
Can be frozen
Serves: 4

Ingredients:
800 g | 28 oz pork (from the shoulder), diced into chunks
400 g | 14 oz can tomatoes
3 tbsp vegetable oil
1 onion, finely chopped
1 clove garlic, finely chopped
2 jalapeño peppers, stem and seeds removed and sliced
1 tbsp tomato puree
600 ml | 21 fl oz | 2 ½ cups chicken stock
1/4 tsp sweet paprika
200 g | 7 oz mixed bell peppers, (red, yellow, green), seeds removed, thickly sliced
150 g | 5 oz green|string beans, trimmed and roughly chopped
300 g | 11 oz tagliatelle
1 tbsp parsley, chopped

To garnish:
basil leaves

Nutritional information:
kcal: 694.6
fat: 25.3 g
saturated fat: 5.7 g

Method:
Blanch the beans in boiling salted water for 3 minutes.

Heat the oil in a large skillet and fry the meat for 5 minutes. Season the pork with salt and ground black pepper.

Add the onions, garlic and jalapeños and fry together for a few minutes.

Pour in the tomatoes, tomato puree and paprika. Bring to a boil, reduce the heat and simmer for 35 minutes.

Add the pepper slices and beans and simmer for a further 10 minutes.

Meanwhile, cook the tagliatelle in boiling salted water according to the instructions on the packet until al dente.

Season the pork and sprinkle with parsley. Serve on plates along with the drained pasta.

Garnish with basil.

Wholemeal tortillas with a chicken and vegetable filling

Prep and cook time: 50 minutes Marinating: 30 minutes Resting: 20 minutes
Cannot be frozen
Serves: 4

Ingredients:

For the tortillas:

200 g | 7 oz 1 $^1/_5$ cups wholemeal flour
1 pinch salt
2 tbsp sunflower oil

For the filling:

4 small chicken breasts, cut into strips
1 tsp hot paprika
2 tbsp olive oil
1 tsp tomato puree
2 red onions, sliced
2 red bell peppers, seeds removed, cut into strips
2 yellow bell peppers

Nutritional information:
kcal: 416.6
fat: 15.2 g
saturated fat: 2.3 g

Method:

To make the tortilla, mix the flour with the salt and oil and 100 ml / 4 fl oz / $^1/_2$ cup of water. Knead into a smooth dough (if necessary add a bit more water). Cover and rest for 20 minutes.

Mix the chicken strips with the paprika and 1 tbsp oil and marinate for 30 minutes.

Once the dough has rested, knead it again on a floured work surface and break into 4 pieces. Roll the pieces out into thin circles (25 cm / 10").

Dry-fry for 1 minute on each side until dark brown speckles appear. As soon as the tortilla inflates turn it over and press down into the skillet. Keep the finished tortillas warm.

Pour the meat and the marinade into a hot, non-stick skillet and fry well on all sides for a few minutes, to brown.

Add the onions and fry for a few minutes, then add the bell peppers, cook for 2 minutes then stir in the tomato puree and fry lightly for a few more minutes.

Spoon some chicken and vegetables onto the tortillas and roll up. Hold in place with wooden toothpicks.

Turkey stir-fry with apricot chutney

Prep and cook time: 1 hour
Can be frozen
Serves: 4

Ingredients:

For the apricot chutney:

1 red chilli pepper, halved, seeds removed, finely chopped
1 onion, roughly chopped
400 g | 14 oz | 2 1/5 cups ripe apricots, peeled, halved, stones removed, cut into pieces
1 untreated lime, zest grated and juiced
2 tbsp honey
2 tbsp apple vinegar
1 tbsp soy sauce
1 tsp fresh root ginger, grated
half tsp cinnamon
1 pinch ground coriander

For the turkey stir-fry:

1 egg
4 - 5 tbsp bread crumbs
2 tsp garam masala
350 g | 12 oz turkey breast, cut into strips
3 tbsp peanut oil
3 red bell pepper, cut into strips
5 spring onions|scallions, cut into thirds

To serve:

naan bread

Nutritional information:

kcal: 424.7
fat: 15.8 g
saturated fat: 2.4 g

Method:

To make the chutney put the chilli pepper, onion and the apricots in a large pot. Add the lime zest and juice, the honey, vinegar, soy sauce, ginger, cinnamon and coriander and bring to a boil.

Leave to simmer for 30 minutes stirring occasionally. Cool until lukewarm.

To make the turkey kebabs beat the egg and season with salt and pepper.

Mix the bread crumbs with the garam masala. Dunk the turkey strips in the egg mixture and then coat in breadcrumbs - make sure the breadcrumbs stick well.

Heat the oil in a high skillet and fry the turkey until golden brown. Add the pepper and spring onions/scallions and fry together for 3 minutes.

Season with salt and pepper and serve with the apricot chutney and naan bread.

Roast turkey with lemon and basil

Prep and cook time: 1 hour 45 minutes Chilling: 5 hours
Can be frozen
Serves: 4

Ingredients:

3 tbsp olive oil
1 onion, chopped
1 garlic clove, crushed
75 g | 1/2 cup white breadcrumbs
6 tbsp fresh basil, chopped
3 lemons, finely grated zest of 2, juice of 3
500 g | 1 lb turkey breast fillet
2 tsp chicken seasoning

Nutritional information:
kcal: 330.2
fat: 11.6 g
saturated fat: 1.8 g

Method:

Heat the oven to 200°C (180°C fan) 400°F, gas 6. To make the stuffing, heat 2 tbsp of olive oil in a skillet and add the onions and garlic, cook gently for 5 minutes until soft but not brown.

Add the breadcrumbs with the lemon zest, stir for a couple of minutes. Season. Add the juice of 2 lemons and the basil. Cool.

To stuff the turkey lay a large sheet of foil on a chopping board, Arrange 10 x 6" lengths of string horizontally across the foil.

Position the turkey breast in the centre, lengthways. Cut a deep slash down the centre of the turkey breast, along its length.

Spoon the stuffing into this pocket. Wrap the meat and stuffing and tie up at 3/4" intervals with the string to secure.

Keep tying the joint until you get to the end. Sprinkle with the chicken seasoning and season with salt and ground black pepper. Squeeze over the juice of the other lemon.
Wrap tightly in foil and put into a roasting pan.

Roast for 1 hour 20 minutes. Cool completely, then chill for at least 5 hours. Slice to serve.

Grilled tuna steaks with kidney beans and tomato salad

Prep and cook time: 30 minutes
Cannot be frozen
Serves: 4

Ingredients:
1 shallot, peeled and finely chopped
2 green peppers, finely chopped
3 tomatoes, deseeded and finely chopped
200 g | 7 oz kidney beans (canned), rinsed and drained
3 tbsp olive oil
1 lime, juice and zest
4 filleted tuna steaks
1 garlic clove, finely chopped
1 tsp finely chopped parsley
1 tbsp fresh lemon balm, chopped

To garnish:
lemon balm leaves
4 lime wedges

Nutritional information:
kcal: 369.5
fat: 18.1 g
saturated fat: 3.6 g

Method:

Mix together the beans, shallots, peppers, tomatoes, 1 tbsp olive oil and lime juice in a bowl.

Season with salt and pepper and allow to marinate.

Cut each tuna steak in half.

Mix the garlic together with the remaining olive oil, lime zest and parsley.

Season with salt and pepper.

Brush the fish pieces with the herb/zest mixture and place on a hot grill. Grill, about 1-2 minutes per side (according to taste).

Mix the lemon balm into the bean salad and season to taste.

Arrange the tuna and salad on plates. Garnish with the lemon balm leaves and lime wedges and serve.

Chicken tagine with olives, artichokes and onions

Prep and cook time: 1 hour
Cannot be frozen
Serves: 4

Ingredients:
1 prepared spring chicken 1.2 kg | 2 1/2 lbs, cut into portion-sized pieces
2 tbsp olive oil
4 - 6 small onions
3 garlic cloves, crushed
1 tsp ginger powder
a pinch of saffron
100 g | 3 1/2 oz green olives, stones removed
1 1/2 lemons, cut into thick slices
2 artichokes (canned, drained), quartered
2 tbsp fresh cilantro|coriander leaves, chopped
2 tbsp fresh parsley leaves, chopped

To garnish:
parsley leaves

Nutritional information:
kcal: 429.8
fat: 15.2 g
saturated fat: 3.8 g

Method:
Rub the chicken pieces with salt and ground black pepper. Heat the oil in a large skillet and fry the chicken on all sides, set aside.

Add the onions to the skillet and fry gently for a few minutes. Add the garlic, ginger, saffron and 225ml / 8 fl oz / 1 cup water and stir well.

Add the chicken and turn often until the pieces are completely covered in sauce. Bring to a boil and leave to simmer for about 30 minutes with a lid on.

Add the olives, lemons, artichokes, coriander/cilantro and parsley and simmer for another 15 minutes. Season to taste. When the chicken is done, remove it from the liquid and keep warm. If the sauce is too runny allow to reduce at a slightly higher temperature.

Arrange the chicken and the rest of the ingredients on a preheated platter (tagine) and garnish with parsley.

Grilled chicken breast with cucumber-tomato salsa

Prep and cook time: 40 minutes
Cannot be frozen
Serves: 4

Ingredients:
For the grilled chicken:
4 chicken breasts
1/2 tsp paprika
2 tbsp olive oil

For the tomato salsa:
500 g | 18 oz tomatoes, sliced
1 small cucumber, halved, seeds removed and sliced
1 red onion, sliced
2 - 3 stalks fresh coriander|cilantro
2 tbsp sweet chilli sauce

To garnish:
1 lime, quartered and griddled

Nutritional information:
kcal: 309
fat: 8.4 g
saturated fat: 1.4 g

Method:
Season the chicken breasts with salt, ground black pepper and paprika and drizzle with oil.

Heat a griddle. Add the chicken and cook and for 5 minutes on each side. Insert a knife into the centre, the chicken is ready if the juices run clear.

Meanwhile, mix together the tomatoes, cucumbers, onions, coriander/cilantro, and chilli sauce. Stir and season with salt and ground black pepper.

Serve the grilled chicken on plates, topped with the tomato salsa.

Garnish with griddled lime and serve with crusty bread.

Asian cashew nut and chicken stir-fry

Prep and cook time: 55 minutes
Cannot be frozen
Serves: 4

Ingredients:
250 g | 9 oz | 1 $^{2}/_{5}$ cups Basmati rice
1 egg
3 tbsp soy sauce
1 tbsp cornflour|cornstarch
600 g | 21 oz chicken breast, finely chopped
2 tbsp peanut oil
200 g | 7 oz | 1 $^{1}/_{3}$ cups lightly salted cashew nuts
1 garlic clove, finely chopped

To garnish:
1 spring onion|scallion, cut into thin strips

Nutritional information:
kcal: 775.3
fat: 32.1 g
saturated fat: 6.6 g

Method:
Cook the rice according to the directions on the packet.

Mix the egg, soy sauce and cornflour/cornstarch into a smooth paste. Season with white pepper, add the chicken and marinate.

Heat 1 tsp oil in a wok and fry the cashew nuts until they are just brown. Pat dry with kitchen paper.

Heat the remaining oil in the wok and fry the meat in small portions at a high temperature. Remove onto a plate.

Once all the meat has been fried, turn the temperature down to a medium heat and fry together the chicken, cashew nuts and garlic. Stirring continuously allow everything to simmer for 5 minutes.

Divide the rice into 4 bowls and add the chicken. Alternatively serve the rice and chicken in separate bowls. Garnish with the chopped spring onions/scallions.

Baked aubergines with a mince and tomato filling

Prep and cook time: 1 hour
Cannot be frozen
Serves: 4

Ingredients:
2 aubergines|eggplants cut in half lengthways
2 tbsp olive oil
1 onion, finely chopped
1 garlic clove, finely chopped
½ tsp dried oregano
½ tsp dried thyme
4 tbsp breadcrumbs
80 g | 3 oz fresh Parmesan cheese, grated
300 g | 11 oz ground beef
1 egg, lightly beaten

For the tomato sauce:
2 tbsp olive oil
1 onion, roughly chopped
2 garlic cloves, roughly chopped
500 g | 18 oz canned chopped tomatoes
1 pinch sugar

To garnish:
4 tomatoes, seeds removed, finely chopped
basil

Nutritional information:
kcal: 512.7
fat: 24.8 g
saturated fat: 5 g

Method:
Heat the oven to 220°C (200°C fan) 400°F, gas 6.

Boil the aubergines/eggplants for 2–3 minutes, covered in salt water.

Hollow out the aubergine/eggplant halves leaving 1 cm around the edge. Lay side by side in an oven-proof dish. Finely chop the flesh and press in a sieve to squeeze out any liquid.

Heat 2 tbsp oil in a skillet and fry the onion and garlic. Add the aubergine/eggplant flesh, oregano and thyme and fry for 5 minutes on a medium heat. Tip into large bowl.

Add the breadcrumbs, 4 tbsp Parmesan cheese, the ground beef and the egg. Season with salt and ground black pepper and mix everything together.

Fill the eggplant halves with the meaty mixture and sprinkle each one with 1 tbsp Parmesan cheese. Cook in the preheated oven for 15–20 minutes.

Heat 2 tbsp oil and fry the onion and garlic. Add the canned tomatoes and bring to a boil. Simmer covered for 10 minutes. Season with salt, sugar and ground black pepper.

Arrange the filled aubergine/eggplant halves on plates and sprinkle with the chopped tomatoes. Serve on the tomato sauce garnished with basil.

Fettuccine with chicken

Prep and cook time: 30 minutes
Can be frozen
Serves: 4

Ingredients:
4 chicken breasts
1/2 tsp peppercorns
1 bay leaf
1 piece lemon zest
400 g | 14 oz fettuccine
1 shallot, finely chopped
1 tbsp olive oil
2 tsp curry powder
2 tbsp fresh parsley, chopped

To garnish:
8 lettuce leaves

Nutritional information:
kcal: 316.3
fat: 7.3 g
saturated fat: 1.2 g

Method:
Place the chicken in a pot with boiling water that is seasoned with salt, peppercorns, bay leaf and lemon zest.
Simmer for 20 minutes.

Cook the fettuccine in boiling salted water, according to packet instructions until al dente.

Remove the cooked chicken from the liquid and cut into bite-size pieces.

Fry the chicken and shallot in the hot olive oil and season with salt, curry powder and ground black pepper.

Drain the pasta. Mix it with the chicken and half of the parsley

Arrange on 4 plates garnished with the lettuce leaves and the remaining parsley.

Potato curry with courgette and cashew nuts

Prep and cook time: 25 minutes
Can be frozen
Serves: 4

Ingredients:
800 g | 28 oz | potatoes, chopped
2 tbsp olive oil
400 g | 14 oz | 3 1/4 cups courgette|zucchini, finely chopped
1 clove garlic, finely chopped
1 onion, finely chopped
1 tbsp root ginger, finely chopped
1 tbsp curry powder
1 tsp cumin
250 g | 9 oz 1 1/3 cups tomatoes, cut into eighths, seeds removed
400 ml | 14 fl oz | 1 2/3 cups vegetable stock
1 tbsp cornflour|cornstarch
60 g | 2 oz cashew nuts

To garnish:
1 tsp cumin seeds

Nutritional information:
kcal: 355.2
fat: 14.5 g
saturated fat: 4.9 g

Method:

Blanch the potatoes in boiling salted water for 8 minutes then drain.

Heat oil and fry the potatoes for a few minutes to brown. Add the courgette/zucchini and fry lightly.

Add the garlic, onion and ginger and season with curry powder, cumin, salt and ground black pepper. Add the tomatoes and vegetable stock and simmer for 15–20 minutes.

Mix the cornflour/cornstarch with a little cold water and stir into the hot curry. Bring to a boil and allow to thicken, then season.

Dry fry the cashew nuts. Sprinkle them over the curry and serve garnished with cumin seeds.

Courgette and feta frittata

Prep and cook time: 35 minutes
Cannot be frozen
Serves: 4

Ingredients:

3 courgettes|zucchinis, quartered lengthways and cut into 4 cm thick pieces
1 tsp olive oil
3 eggs
2 cloves garlic
250 ml | 9 fl oz | 1 cup semi-skimmed milk
200 g | 7 oz | 1 1/3 cups feta
2 tbsp fresh mint, chopped
1 tbsp fresh parsley
for the garnish
mint sprigs

Nutritional information:
kcal: 269.7
fat: 18.4 g
saturated fat: 6.1 g

Method:

Heat the oven to 180°C (160°C fan) 375°F, gas 5.

Brush an 8" round tin with the oil and lay the corgette/zucchini pieces in it.

Put the eggs, garlic, milk, feta, mint and parsley in a blender and puree quickly.

Season with salt and ground black pepper and pour over the courgettes/zucchinis.

Bake in the preheated oven for 20 minutes until golden brown.

Remove from the oven, place a plate over the top and upturn the frittata onto a dish.

Serve garnished with mint.

Tagliatelle with spinach and Roquefort

Prep and cook time: 30 minutes
Cannot be frozen
Serves: 4

Ingredients:
400 g | 14 oz tagliatelle
1 onion, finely chopped
1 garlic clove, finely chopped
1 tbsp olive oil
200 ml | 7 fl oz | 4/5 cups vegetable stock
50 g | 2 oz Roquefort
250 g | 9 oz | 8 1/3 cups young spinach, roughly chopped

Nutritional information:
kcal: 458.7
fat: 16.3 g
saturated fat: 3.8 g

Method:

Cook the pasta in boiling salted water, for about 10 minutes until al dente.

Heat the oil and fry the onion and garlic for a few minutes to soften but not colour.

Pour in the stock. Add the Roquefort and simmer until slightly creamy, stirring occasionally.

Arrange the drained pasta onto plates and sprinkle the fresh spinach on top. Season with salt and ground black pepper.

Pour the sauce over the pasta and serve.

Herb, cream cheese and courgette lasagne

Prep and cook time: 40 minutes
Cannot be frozen
Serves: 4

Ingredients:
10 - 12 lasagne sheets
3 courgettes|zucchinis, cut lengthways into thin slices
300 g | 2/3 cup low-fat cream cheese
150 ml | 2/3 cup sour cream
50 g mixed herbs, (parsley, chives, dill, basil, mint), finely chopped
2 garlic cloves, finely chopped

To garnish:
mint leaves

Nutritional information:
kcal: 310.7
fat: 6.3 g
saturated fat: 3 g

Method:

Cook the lasagne sheets in boiling salt water until al dente. Remove from the water one by one, drain and lay next to each other on tin foil to cool.

Blanch the courgettes/zucchinis in boiling salted water for one minute and refresh with ice cold water.

Mix the cream cheese and the sour cream. Add salt, ground black pepper, the herbs and mix in the garlic. Season well.

Lay 2–3 lasagne sheets widthways on a plate, slightly overlapping. Spread the cheese mixture on top and arrange the courgettes/zucchinis slices on top overlapping each slice over the previous one.

Repeat this procedure until all ingredients are used up and the upper layer is made up of courgette/zucchini.

Garnish with mint leaves.

salads.

Lentil-pepper salad with rocket

Prep and cook time: 1 hour
Cannot be frozen
Serves: 4

Ingredients:
300 g | 11 oz beluga lentils, soaked overnight
4 red bell pepper, halved
3 tbsp olive oil
2 garlic cloves, finely chopped
2 tbsp balsamic vinegar
2 handfuls rocket|arugula
2 tbsp Parmesan cheese shavings

Nutritional information:
kcal: 414.2
fat: 14.9 g
saturated fat: 2.7 g

Method:
Heat the oven to 220°C (200°C fan) 425°F, gas 7.

Cook the lentils in salted water until they are soft, this will take about 45 minutes.

Meanwhile, place the bell pepper halves skin side up on a cookie sheet lined with non-stick paper. Roast in the hot oven for 10 minutes or until the skin starts to blister and turn black.

Remove from the oven and put into a plastic bag and seal.

When the peppers are cool remove the skin and cut the pepper into strips.

Heat the oil in a skillet and lightly fry the pepper. Add the garlic and continue to fry for a further few minutes.

Drain the lentils and add the balsamic vinegar. Season with salt and ground black pepper.

Spoon the warm lentils onto plates. Top with peppers and then add a handful of rocket/arugula and finish with Parmesan shavings.

Thai chicken noodle salad

Prep and cook time: 35 minutes
Cannot be frozen
Serves: 4

Ingredients:

2 large skinless chicken breasts
75 g | 2 ½ oz dried medium egg noodles
100 g | 3 ½ oz dried rice noodles
2 good handfuls of baby spinach leaves
2 carrots, cut into thin strips
half cucumber, halved lengthways and sliced
4 spring onions|scallions, finely sliced
1 red pepper, seeded and finely sliced
1 yellow pepper, seeded and finely sliced
1 tbsp coriander|cilantro leaves, chopped
1 red chilli, seeds removed and finely chopped
2 garlic cloves, finely chopped
1 tbsp root ginger, finely chopped
2 tbsp soy sauce
juice of 1 lime
2 tbsp olive oil

Nutritional information:
kcal: 417.3
fat: 7.9 g
saturated fat: 1.3 g

Method:

Heat the broiler (grill) to high. Put the chicken on the grill pan and cook for 10-12 minutes.

Meanwhile, cook the egg and rice noodles according to pack instructions. Drain and run cold water through to stop them sticking together. Put into 4 bowls.

Sprinkle over the carrots, cucumber, spring onions/scallions, red and yellow peppers.

Thinly slice the chicken and add to the bowl, sprinkled with coriander/cilantro leaves and chilli.

Mix the garlic, ginger, soy sauce, lime juice and olive oil with 2 tablespoons water.

Pour into mini bowls, arrange on top of salad bowls. Pour over the salad and toss well to serve.

Tomatoes filled with couscous and shrimp salad

Prep and cook time: 20 minutes
Cannot be frozen
Serves: 4 (12 tomatoes)

Ingredients:

50 ml | 1 3/4 fl oz | 1/5 cups white wine
200 ml | 7 fl oz | 4/5 cups vegetable stock
120 g | 4 oz | 3/4 cup couscous
12 tomatoes, tops cut off and retained
1 green bell pepper, seeds removed and finely chopped
1 red bell pepper, seeds removed and finely chopped
1 garlic clove, finely chopped
2 tbsp fresh dill, chopped
3 tbsp olive oil
100 g | 3 1/2 oz | 1/3 cup prepared prawns|shrimps
1 tsp lemon juice

Nutritional information:
kcal: 246.6
fat: 15.8 g
saturated fat: 2.5 g

Method:

Bring the white wine and the stock to a boil. Pour it over the couscous and let soak for 5 minutes. Mix with a fork.

Hollow out the tomatoes.

Mix the couscous with the bell peppers, garlic, dill and olive oil. Add the prawns/shrimps and season with lemon juice, salt and ground black pepper.

Fill the tomatoes with the couscous and place the tomato top "lid" on top to serve.

Rice salad with lentils, aubergines and a garlic dressing

Prep and cook time: 1 hour
Cannot be frozen
Serves: 4

Ingredients:
300 g | 11 oz 1½ cup long grain and wild rice
1 tbsp olive oil
1 aubergine|eggplant, cut into small pieces
1 red bell pepper, seeds removed, cut into pieces
3 spring onions|scallions, cut into strips
200 g | 7 oz 1 ¼ cups brown canned lentils, drained
1 tbsp parsley, chopped

For the garlic dressing:
4 cloves garlic, chopped
4 tbsp olive oil
juice of 1 lemon
1 pinch of sugar

Nutritional information:
kcal: 637.2
fat: 20.3 g
saturated fat: 2.4 g

Method:

Cook the long grain and wild rice according to the directions on the packet.

Heat the oil in a large skillet and fry the aubergine/eggplant for 5 minutes until golden brown.

Add the bell pepper, reduce the heat, cover and simmer for 3 minutes.

Add the spring onions/scallions.

Drain the rice and rinse with cold water.

Add the rice and the lentils to the aubergine/eggplant and peppers and season with salt and ground black pepper. Cool.

To make the garlic dressing; put the garlic into a jam jar. Add the olive oil, lemon juice, 4 tbsp water, sugar, salt and black pepper. Shake to mix.

Arrange the rice salad on plates, garnish with parsley and serve with the garlic dressing.

Chicken and avocado salad

Prep and cook time: 25 minutes
Cannot be frozen
Serves: 4

Ingredients:
4 chicken breasts
5 tbsp oil
3 tbsp balsamic vinegar
4 tomatoes, halved and sliced
60 g | 2 oz black olives, pitted and sliced
2 red onions, peeled and cut into rings
2 avocados, halved, pitted and peeled
juice of half a lemon
20 g | 3/4 oz basil leaves

Nutritional information:
kcal: 513.8
fat: 37.2 g
saturated fat: 5.8 g

Method:
Season the chicken with salt and ground black pepper.

Heat 1 tbsp oil in a skillet and fry the chicken for 10 minutes, turning, until golden-brown.

To make the dressing, mix the rest of the olive oil with the balsamic vinegar with salt and ground black pepper in a jar. Seal and shake to combine.

Mix together the tomatoes, olives and onions.

Slice the avocados and immediately sprinkle with lemon juice.

Mix all the salad ingredients into the salad dressing and serve on plates.

Take the chicken breast out of the skillet, cut into pieces and arrange on top of the salad with the basil leaves.

Sole rolls on a lentil salad

Prep and cook time: 50 minutes
Cannot be frozen
Serves: 4

Ingredients:

For the lentil salad:

300 g | 11 oz | 1 ½ cups dried beluga lentils

1 tsp fennel seeds

600 ml | 21 fl oz | 2 ½ cups vegetable stock

1 carrot, finely chopped

1 stick celery, finely chopped; leaves set aside for garnish

1 small yellow courgette|zucchini, finely chopped

1 onion, finely chopped

For the fish:

8 sole fillets, 70 g|2 ½ oz each

4 tbsp lemon juice

2 tbsp olive oil

2 shallots, finely chopped

150 ml | 5 fl oz | ⅔ cup dry white wine

50 g | 1 ¾ oz | ½ cup leek, just the white part, cut into thin strips

2 tomatoes, seeds removed, finely chopped

To garnish:

4 celery leaves

Nutritional information:

kcal: 277

fat: 5.5 g

saturated fat: 0.7 g

Method:

Boil the lentils and the fennel seeds in the stock and simmer for 35–40 minutes until the lentils are soft.

After 25 minutes add the carrots, celery, courgettes/zucchinis and onions to the lentils and cook for 10 more minutes until the lentils and vegetables are tender. Season with salt and ground black pepper. Cover and set aside.

Season the fish with salt and ground black pepper and drizzle with 1 tbsp lemon juice. Roll two fillets up together from the fat end with skin on the inside.

Heat the olive oil and fry the shallots until transparent. Add the rest of the lemon juice, the wine and 3 tbsp water.

Arrange the sole rolls in the pan and bring to a boil.

Sprinkle the leek and tomatoes over the top of the fish, cover and steam for 8 minutes.

Arrange the sole rolls on top of the lentils and serve garnished with the celery leaves.

Thai beef salad with rice noodles

Prep and cook time: 30 minutes
Can be frozen
Serves: 4

Ingredients:
500 g | 18 oz sirloin steak, cut into strips
3 tbsp fish sauce
300 g | 11 oz rice noodles
2 tbsp sesame oil
5 cloves garlic, chopped
2 red chillies, deseeded and chopped
300 g | 11 oz green|string beans, roughly chopped
2 sticks celery, cut into strips
4 tbsp light soy sauce

To garnish:
12 coriander|cilantro leaves
12 lemon balm leaves

Nutritional information:
kcal: 390
fat: 13.1 g
saturated fat: 3.2 g

Method:
Put the meat into a non-metallic dish and season with fish sauce. Leave to marinate for 10 minutes.

Cook the noodles according to packet instructions in plenty of salted water and drain.

Heat the oil in a large frying pan. Quickly stir fry the steak for 3 minutes.

Add the garlic and chilli, green/string beans and celery. Fry over a medium heat for about 3 minutes.

Add the rice noodles and soy sauce, mix well and fry for a further 1-2 minutes.

Serve garnished with coriander/cilantro and lemon balm leaves.

Greek salad

Prep and cook time: 20 minutes
Cannot be frozen
Serves: 4

Ingredients:
1 cucumber, diced
1 green pepper, deseeded and cut into strips
2 tomatoes, diced
1 red onion, sliced
1 romaine lettuce heart, leaves torn into pieces
2 tbsp black olives
2 tbsp green olives
1 clove garlic, crushed
200 g | 7 oz low-fat feta cheese, diced
3 tbsp wine vinegar
3 tbsp olive oil
1 tsp capers
a pinch of sugar
2 tbsp basil, leaves torn

Nutritional information:
kcal: 355
fat: 23.7 g
saturated fat: 4.1 g

Method:

Mix together the peppers, tomatoes, onion and lettuce.

Add the black and green olives, garlic and feta cheese.
Peel the cucumber, halve lengthwise, scrape out the seeds and dice the flesh. Add to the mix.

Put the vinegar and olive oil into a jar, with the caper and a pinch of sugar and season with salt and ground black pepper. Seal and shake to mix.

Toss the dressing into the salads.

Serve sprinkled with basil leaves.

Green bean and lentil salad with feta

Prep and cook time: 25 minutes
Serves: 4

Ingredients:

300 g | 11 oz | 2 3/4 cups green|string beans, halved
1 carrot, finely chopped
1 stick celery, finely chopped
300 g | 11 oz | 1 1/2 cups canned puy lentils, drained
1 tbsp parsley, chopped
1 tbsp chives
4 tbsp olive oil
3 tbsp cider vinegar
150 g | 5 oz | 1 cup feta cheese cubes

Nutritional information:
kcal: 476.7
fat: 15.4 g
saturated fat: 4.8 g

Method:

Boil the beans in salted water for 2 minutes. Add the carrot and the celery and cook for a further 4 minutes.

Drain, and cool under running water then tip into a bowl.

Mix together the vegetables and the lentils. Add the parsley and the chives.

Put the oil, vinegar, salt and ground black pepper into a jar and shake to mix.

Pour the dressing over the lentils and vegetables and mix together.

Top with crumbled feta cheese.

Lukewarm noodle salad with chicken breast and mint

Prep and cook time: 40 minutes
Cannot be frozen
Serves: 4

Ingredients:
400 g | 14 oz egg noodles
4 chicken breasts, chopped
3 tbsp sunflower oil
1 tsp fresh root ginger, grated
1 chilli, halved, deseeded and finely chopped
2 tbsp soy sauce
100 ml | 3 1/2 fl oz | 2/5 cups chicken stock
1/2 cucumber, seeds removed, cut into thin strips 8 cm long
100 g | 3 1/2 | oz 1 cup fresh bean sprouts
2 tbsp mint, roughly chopped

Nutritional information:
kcal: 569.1
fat: 11.9 g
saturated fat: 1.7 g

Method:
Cook the noodles in salted water according to packet instructions until al dente.

Meanwhile, fry the ginger and chilli in hot oil for 1 minute and then add the meat. Season ground black pepper, fry lightly and then pour in the soy sauce and the stock. Remove from the heat and allow to rest for a few minutes.

Drain and rinse the noodles.

Put into a bowl together with the chicken, cucumber and bean sprouts. Stir in the mint.

Serve lukewarm.

Lobster with avocado, grapefruit and beetroot

Prep and cook time: 55 minutes
Cannot be frozen
Serves: 4

Ingredients:
2 lobsters
1 stick celery
1 carrot, chopped
1 onion, chopped
3 stalks parsley
1 bay leaf
2 sprigs thyme
100 ml | 3 ½ fl oz | ⅖ cups dry white wine

for the salad:
2 red beets
2 pink grapefruits
2 avocados, stone removed and sliced
80 g | 3 oz mixed salad leaves, (e.g. radicchio, rocket|arugula, chard)
½ lemon, juiced
2 tbsp olive oil

Nutritional information:
kcal: 366.6
fat: 26.9 g
saturated fat: 3.6 g

Method:

Put 900ml / 30fl oz / 4 cups water and the white wine into a pan and bring to a boil.

Add the celery, carrot, onion, parsley, bay and thyme, season with salt and ground black pepper and simmer for 15 minutes.

Plunge the lobsters head first into the broth and cook for 8-10 minutes, depending on size. Take out and refresh in cold water.

Cut in half lengthwise with a large, sharp knife. Take the meat out of the tails and the claws.

For the salad, steam the red beets for about 30 minutes.

Peel the grapefruits with a sharp knife, removing the white pith and skin, and cut out the segments.

Arrange the avocado and grapefruit attractively (like the petals of a flower) on 4 plates, alternating avocado and grapefruit segments.

Peel and dice the beets. Mix with 1 tbsp olive oil and 1 tbsp lemon juice.

Put a handful of salad leaves in the middle of the plates and arrange the diced beet around the outside. Put the lobster meat in the middle of the plate.

Put one lobster claw and half of the tail on each plate.

Mix the rest of the lemon juice and oil, drizzle over the salad and sprinkle with sea salt before serving.

dips, snacks & tapas.

Potato wedges with yoghurt herb dip

Prep and cook time: 1 hour
Cannot be frozen
Serves: 4

Ingredients:
1kg | 35 oz baking potatoes, cut into wedges
2 tbsp sunflower oil
150 g | 5 oz cucumber, chopped
4 tbsp chives
250 ml | 9 fl oz | 1 1/8 cup Greek yoghurt, low-fat
half a lemon, juiced

To garnish:
2 tbsp cucumber, chopped
4 radishes, chopped
5 chives
2 tbsp parsley, chopped

Nutritional information:
kcal: 361.4
fat: 17.8 g
saturated fat: 5.3 g

Method:
Heat the oven to 220°C (200°C fan) 400°F, gas 6.

Put the potato wedges into a roasting pan, drizzle over the oil and season with salt and ground black pepper.

Roast for 20 minutes, turn and cook for 20 more minutes until golden-brown.

Mix together most of the cucumber, radishes and chives, all of the yoghurt and lemon juice and season with salt and ground black pepper.

Spoon into a bowl and garnish with the remaining cucumber, radishes and chives.

Finally sprinkle the chopped parsley over the potato wedges and serve them with the dip.

Turkey and sausage kebabs served with a yoghurt dip

Prep and cook time: 50 minutes
Cannot be frozen
Serves: 4

Ingredients:
1 courgette|zucchini, trimmed and sliced
24 cherry tomatoes
12 shallots
4 sausages, cut into bite size pieces
300 g | 11 oz turkey breast, cut into bite-size pieces
oil, for brushing
1 tsp fresh marjoram, chopped
1 tsp fresh rosemary needles
parsley, to garnish
8 kebab sticks

For the yoghurt dip:
300 g | 11 oz yoghurt
1 tbsp lemon juice
50 g | 2 oz cucumber, peeled and finely chopped
50 g | 2 oz radishes, sliced
2 tbsp garden cress
1 tbsp chives, chopped

To garnish:
flat parsley

Nutritional information:
kcal: 541.6
fat: 40.8 g
saturated fat: 15.2 g

Method:

Thread courgettes/zucchinis, tomatoes, shallots, sausages and turkey in any order onto the kebab sticks. Season with salt and ground black pepper and brush with oil.

Grill for about 6–8 minutes on a hot barbecue, turning it as needed.

Serve sprinkled with the marjoram and rosemary, garnish with parsley and accompany with the yoghurt dip.

To make the dip, mix the yoghurt with the lemon juice, season with salt and pepper and divide into small bowls.

Sprinkle over the cucumber, radishes, chives and garden cress.

Serve with kebabs and garnish with parsley.

Couscous porridge

Prep and cook time: 15 minutes
Cannot be frozen
Serves: 4

Ingredients:
400 ml | 14 fl oz | 1 2/3 cups apple juice, heated
400 g | 14 oz | 2 1/3 cups couscous
3 soft pears, pips removed and finely chopped
2 tbsp honey
juice of 1 lemon
1 pinch cinnamon

To garnish:
4 sprigs mint

Nutritional information:
kcal: 447.3
fat: 1.4
saturated fat: 0.2

Method:
Pour the hot apple juice over the couscous and let the couscous absorb the juice for 5 minutes, stirring occasionally.

Place the pears in a pot with the honey, lemon juice and cinnamon and bring to a boil.

Remove from the heat and mix in with the couscous.

Serve in bowls garnished with mint leaves.

Mediterranean baked stuffed onions

Prep and cook time: 1 hour
Cannot be frozen
Serves: 4

Ingredients:

2 tbsp wheat grains
4 large Bermuda|Spanish onions, peeled
1 small courgette|zucchini, trimmed and finely chopped
2 spring onions|scallions, chopped
1 small aubergine|eggplant, finely chopped
3 tbsp | 1/8 cup olive oil
2 sprigs fresh tarragon, leaves removed
1 shallot, peeled and finely chopped
1 garlic clove, peeled and finely chopped
800g chopped tomatoes
20 g | 3/4 oz fresh basil, roughly chopped
30 g | 1 oz Gouda cheese, sliced

Nutritional information:
kcal: 212.7
fat: 10.9 g
saturated fat: 2.5 g

Method:

Heat the oven to 200°C (180°C fan) 400°F, gas 6.

Boil the wheat grains in salted water for 20 minutes, until just tender, then drain.

Meanwhile, cook the onions in salted water for 10–15 minutes depending on their size.

Remove from the water and dry onions. Cut the tops off and carefully hollow out the flesh using a teaspoon.

Roughly chop 2 tbsp of the onion flesh.

Heat 2 tbsp oil in a very large skillet and fry the onion flesh, courgette/zucchini, spring onions/scallions, aubergine/eggplant for 10 minutes to soften.

Add the tarragon and season with salt and ground black pepper.

Heat remaining oil in a skillet and fry the shallot and the garlic in until transparent. Add the tomatoes and simmer for 10 minutes.

Add most of the basil leaving some aside for the garnish, season with salt and ground pepper and stir.

Fill the large onions with the vegetables and sprinkle the wheat grains over the top.

Pour the tomato sauce into an oven-proof dish and place the stuffed onions on top.

Place a slice of Gouda on each onion and bake for 20 minutes until golden-brown.

Turkey wrap

Prep and cook time: 35 minutes Rest: 15 minutes
Cannot be frozen
Serves: 4

Ingredients:
200 g | 7 oz wholemeal flour
1 tbsp lemon juice
3 tbsp olive oil
dash of Tabasco
4 lettuce leaves
4 slices turkey
2 tomatoes, seeds removed, cut into strips
60 g | 2 oz Cheddar cheese, grated
1 red onion, chopped

Nutritional information:
kcal: 368.2
fat: 18.1 g
saturated fat: 5.8 g

Method:
Mix the flour, with a pinch salt and 100 ml / 4l oz / 1/2 cup lukewarm water and knead until a soft dough is formed and it is no longer sticky (add a little more water, if needed). Cover and allow to rest for 15 minutes.

Next, divide the dough into 4 equal pieces. Roll out on a floured work surface into circle 20 cm / 8".

Dry-fry in a non-stick skillet until dark brown speckles appear on both sides. Keep the wraps warm.

Mix the lemon juice with the olive oil, a few drops of Tabasco, salt and ground black pepper to make a salad dressing.

Cover the wraps with lettuce, turkey, tomatoes, cheese and onions and drizzle with the dressing.

Roll up and serve cut in halves.

Potato tortilla with ham and kidney beans

Prep and cook time: 50 minutes
Cannot be frozen
Serves: 4

Ingredients:

2 tbsp olive oil

500 g | 18 oz | 3 cups baking potatoes, finely chopped

1 onion, cut into rings

4 eggs

4 tbsp sour cream

1 tbsp fresh parsley, chopped

200 g | 7 oz | 3/4 cup tinned kidney beans, drained and washed

100 g | 3 1/2 oz | 2/5 cup tinned sweetcorn kernels, drained and washed

6 thin slices ham, cut into strips

Nutritional information:

kcal: 443.1

fat: 21.3 g

saturated fat: 5.7 g

Method:

Heat the olive oil in a skillet and fry the potatoes for 10 minutes.

Add the onion and fry gently for a further 5 minutes, stirring occasionally, until the potatoes soften. Season with salt and ground black pepper.

Whisk together the eggs, sour cream and parsley and season with salt and ground black pepper.

Pour the egg mixture over the potatoes, sprinkle on the sweetcorn kernels and the beans and lay the ham strips on top.

Cook for 10 minutes until firm. Brown the top under a preheated grill.

Cut into 4 pieces and serve garnished with lettuce.

Penne alla ragusana

Prep and cook time: 25 minutes
Cannot be frozen
Serves: 4

Ingredients:
2 tbsp olive oil
2 cloves garlic, finely chopped
1 chilli pepper, halved, seeds removed and finely chopped
500 g | 18 oz | 2 2/2 cups chopped tomatoes
100 ml | 3 1/2 fl oz | 7 tbsp dry red wine
400 g | 14 oz | 4 cups penne pasta
2 tbsp parsley, roughly chopped
3 tbsp capers
2 tbsp pitted black olives, chopped
1 tbsp lemon juice
1 pinch sugar

To garnish:
1 tbsp roughly chopped parsley leaves

Nutritional information:
kcal: 416
fat: 13.07 g
saturated fat: 2.1 g

Method:
Heat the oil in large skillet and for 30 seconds. Add the tomatoes and wine and simmer uncovered for a 10 minutes.

Meanwhile cook the pasta in salted water until al dente for 10 minutes.

Add the parsley, capers and olives to the sauce and season with salt ground black pepper, lemon juice and sugar.

Drain the pasta, mix with the sauce and serve.

Garnish with parsley.

Chestnut burgers with a potato and lamb's lettuce salad

Prep and cook time: 1 hour 15 minutes
Cannot be frozen
Serves: 4

Ingredients:

400 g | 1 lb baking potatoes
1 tbsp olive oil
1 shallot, finely chopped
100 g | 4/5 canned chestnuts, roughly chopped
300 g | 3/4 lb ground rosé veal
1 egg
4 tbsp parsley, chopped
2 tbsp sunflower oil
100 ml | 1/3 cup chicken stock
2 tbsp red wine vinegar
1 tbsp walnut oil
150 g lamb's lettuce
1 red onion, cut into rings

Nutritional information:
kcal: 329.2
fat: 15.7
saturated fat: 3.4

Method:

Cook the potatoes for 25-30 minutes in salt water until tender. Drain and cool.

Heat the olive oil and fry the shallot and the chestnuts until the shallots turn translucent. Remove from the heat and tip into a bowl.

Add the veal, egg, 2 tbsp parsley, salt and ground black pepper and mix to form a smooth dough.

Shape into 4 burgers.

Heat the sunflower oil and fry the burgers on both sides for 5 minutes until golden brown.

Remove from the skillet and roll the sides with the remaining parsley.

Add the stock to skillet, warm and season with salt and ground black pepper.

Mix the potatoes with the vinegar, walnut oil, salt and ground black pepper. Mix in the lettuce and the onion rings and arrange on a plate.

Place the burgers on the plate and drizzle with the stock to serve.

Saffron pilau with cashew nuts and raisins

Prep and cook time: 25 minutes
Cannot be frozen
Serves: 4

Ingredients:
400 g | 14 oz | 2 cups Basmati rice, rinsed
2 tsp oil
75 g | 2 ½ oz | ½ cup cashew nuts
1 tbsp rose water
1 pinch saffron threads
1 medium onion, finely chopped
75 g | 2 ½ oz | half cup raisins
900 ml | 32 fl oz | 4 cups chicken stock

To garnish:
4 tbsp natural yoghurt
1 spring onion|scallion, diagonally sliced

Nutritional information:
kcal: 695.2
fat: 21.9 g
saturated fat: 4.2 g

Method:
Heat a skillet and dry fry the cashew nuts for a few minutes until golden brown. Place in a bowl.

Put the rose water in a bowl and soften the saffron threads in it.

Fry the onions in the oil until transparent. Add the raisins and the rose water and saffron and fry for approximately 2 minutes.

Heat the chicken stock in a large pot. Add the rice and bring to a boil. Cover and simmer on a low heat for 15 minutes.

Turn off the heat and place a folded kitchen towel between the pot and the lid and let the rice steam like this for 5 minutes. Then remove from the heat completely and allow to steep for a further 5 minutes.

Stir in the onions and raisins and the cashew nuts.

Divide the pilau into 4 bowls and garnish with a dollop of yoghurt and the spring onions/scallions.

Courgette omelette

Prep and cook time: 20 minutes
Cannot be frozen
Serves: 4

Ingredients:
2 tbsp olive oil
2 large courgettes|zucchinis, thinly sliced lengthways
8 eggs
5 tbsp milk
3 tbsp finely grated Parmesan
16 parsley leaves
16 basil leaves

Nutritional information:
kcal: 407.7
fat: 28.5 g
saturated fat: 6.6 g

Method:
Heat 1 tbsp oil in a frying pan and fry the courgettes/zucchinis slices on both sides until golden brown.

Whisk the eggs with the milk, salt, pepper and Parmesan.

Heat 1 tsp oil into a non-stick frying pan and pour in one quarter of the egg mixture and cook for 2 minutes until the base is firm to make a flat omelette (without folding).
Keep warm.

Repeat to make 3 more omelettes.

Put the omelettes on plates and top with the courgette slices. Season with salt and pepper, garnish with basil and parsley leaves and serve immediately.

Baked potatoes with ham served on zucchini quark

Prep and cook time: 1 hour
Serves: 4

Ingredients:

2 large, floury potatoes, peeled and halved
4 tbsp olive oil
1 large courgette|zucchini, diced
250 g | 9 oz | 1 cup quark (low-fat soft cheese)
1 tbsp parsley, chopped
1 clove garlic, crushed
4 slices of Serrano or Parma ham

Nutritional information:
kcal: 384.1
fat: 6.6 g
saturated fat: 0.9 g

Method:

Heat the oven to 200°C (180°C fan) 400°F, gas 6.

Lay the potatoes cut side down, on a baking sheet sprinkled with 1 tbsp olive oil and a pinch of salt. Bake for 45 minutes.

Cook the courgettes/zucchinis in a little salted water for 3 minutes, then refresh in cold water and drain.

Stir the quark until smooth and season with salt and ground black pepper. Stir in the courgettes/zucchinis.

Put the parsley, garlic, a pinch of salt and 3 tbsp olive oil into the blender and blend to a fine puree.

Shortly before the potatoes are cooked, fry the slices of ham in a non-stick pan on both sides 1-2 minutes until crisp.

Spoon the quark mix on to plates, drizzle with parsley oil, put the potatoes on top and finish with the Serrano or Parma ham.

Vitamin bomb: beetroot fruit drink

Prep and cook time: 10 minutes
Cannot be frozen
Serves: 4 (glasses of 150ml)

Ingredients:
6 tbsp crushed ice
juice of 4 oranges
250 ml | 9 fl oz | 1 cup beetroot|beet juice, unsweetened
1 - 2 tbsp runny honey

To garnish:
8 slices orange
4 bamboo sticks

Nutritional information:
kcal: 61.5
fat: 0.2 g
saturated fat: 0.0 g

Method:

Divide the crushed ice between 4 glasses.

Strain the orange juice into a jug, then pour into the beetroot/beet juice and honey. Mix it thoroughly.

Pour the juice over the crushed ice and fill up with sparkling mineral water.

Skewer the orange slices onto the bamboo sticks

Garnish the glasses with the orange sticks.

Sole and salmon rolls with spinach

Prep and cook time: 30 minutes
Cannot be frozen
Serves: 4

Ingredients:

8 sole fillets, 80 g | 3 oz each
150 g | 5 oz smoked salmon, sliced
100 g | 3 1/2 oz baby spinach leaves, finely chopped
400 g | 14 oz baby spinach leaves
200 ml | 7 fl oz | 4/5 cups fish stock
200 ml | 7 fl oz | 4/5 cups white wine

Nutritional information:
kcal: 201.6
fat: 5 g
saturated fat: 1 g

Method:

Open out the sole fillets and season with salt and freshly ground black pepper.

Place the smoked salmon slices on top of the sole fillets.

Sprinkle over the chopped spinach on top of the smoked salmon and season with ground black pepper.

Roll the fillets up, securing with a toothpick, and arrange in a steamer.

Pour the fish stock and white wine into a pan and bring to the boil.

Rest the steamer over a pan and arrange the rest of the spinach leaves around the fish.

Cover and steam for 6 minutes until the fish is tender and flakes easily.

Chicken satay & avocado salad

Prep and cook time: 45 minutes Marinating: 1 hour
Cannot be frozen
Serves: 4

Ingredients:

For the kebabs:

- 2 tbsp honey
- 1 pinch chilli flakes
- 4 tbsp soy sauce
- 1 tbsp turmeric
- 1 tsp fresh ginger, grated
- 4 tbsp peanut oil
- 600 g | 21 oz chicken breast, cut into thin strips

For the sauce:

- 1 shallot, very finely chopped
- 1 garlic clove, very finely chopped
- 1 tsp sugar
- 150 ml | 5 fl oz | 2/3 cups low-fat coconut milk
- 2 tbsp peanut butter

For the salad:

- 1 large avocado
- 1 red bell pepper, halved, seeds and interior white skin removed, finely chopped
- 1 lemon, juice
- Cayenne pepper

Nutritional information:

kcal: 528.08
fat: 31.1 g
saturated fat: 4.8 g

Method:

To make the kebabs mix the honey, chilli flakes, soy sauce, turmeric and ginger with 2 tbsp peanut oil add the chicken, stir and marinate for at least an hour.

To make the sauce, heat the oil and fry the shallot and the garlic for a couple of minutes or until soft. Sprinkle with sugar and caramelise until dark brown.

Add the coconut milk, heat and then add the peanut butter, allowing it to melt. Season with salt and pepper.

To make the salad, mix the avocado and the pepper together. Pour the lemon juice over the top, season with salt and ground black pepper and sprinkle with Cayenne pepper.

Skewer the chicken onto the kebab sticks in a wave-like motion, drizzle with the remaining 2 tbsp oil and grill for 8 minutes, turning as needed.

Spoon the peanut sauce onto 4 plates and arrange the 2 kebabs on top. Serve with the avocado salad.

Pork and courgette bake

Prep and cook time: 30 minutes
Can be frozen
Serves: 4

Ingredients:
1 garlic clove, finely chopped
1 onion, finely chopped
2 tbsp vegetable oil
400 g | 1 lb ground beef
1 tbsp flour
225 ml | 1 cup vegetable stock
100 g | 1/2 cup frozen peas
2 tomatoes, finely chopped
1 tsp fresh root ginger, grated
1 tbsp curry powder
250 g | 2 cups courgettes|zucchinis, finely chopped
200 g | 1 1/2 cups boiled potatoes, finely sliced

Nutritional information:
kcal: 343.2
fat: 18.1 g
saturated fat: 5.6 g

Method:
Heat the oven to 200°C (180°C in a fan oven) 400°F, gas 6.

Fry the onion and the garlic in hot oil. Add the ground beef and fry until crumbly. Dust with flour and pour on the stock.

Bring to a boil, add the peas and remove from the heat. Add the tomatoes and season well with salt, ground black pepper, ginger and curry powder.

Mix half the courgette/zucchini with the potatoes and press firmly into four small baking dishes. Press the meat mixture firmly on top making sure to include some of the juices.

Put the remaining courgette/zucchini pieces on the top and sprinkle with curry powder. Bake in the preheated oven for 20 minutes.

Pork fillet with a red pepper dip

Prep and cook time: 40 minutes
Cannot be frozen
Serves: 4

Ingredients:
1 tbsp hot mustard
1 tsp tomato puree
600 g | 21 oz pork fillet, cut into 12 pieces
chilli flakes
2 tbsp olive oil

For the dip:
1 red bell pepper, seeds removed and finely chopped
150 g | 5 oz | good $1/2$ cup low-fat cream cheese
2 tbsp white wine vinegar
5 tbsp orange juice

For the salad:
2 stick celery, cut into strips lengthways
150 g | 5 oz | 7 $1/2$ cups rocket|arugula
2 tbsp olive oil
3 tbsp white balsamic vinegar

Nutritional information:
kcal: 312
fat: 13.5 g
saturated fat: 2.6 g

Method:

Mix the mustard and the tomato puree and brush the pork with the mixture.

Season with salt, ground black pepper and chilli flakes.

Heat the oil for 5 minutes and fry the pork fillets until golden brown.

Meanwhile make the dip: mix the bell pepper with the cream cheese, vinegar and orange juice and season with salt and ground black pepper.

To make the salad, mix the celery and the rocket/arugula.

Pour the olive oil into a jar and add the white balsamic vinegar, 2 tbsp water, salt and ground black pepper. Shake to combine and drizzle over the salad.

Arrange everything in bowls and serve.

Focaccia verde – with asparagus and courgette

Prep and cook time: 40 minutes Rising: 30 minutes
Cannot be frozen
Serves: 4

Ingredients:
For the dough:
125 g | 4 1/2 oz | 1/2 cup low -fat cream cheese
3 tbsp olive oil
1 egg
250 g | 9 oz 1 | 2/3 cup flour
half tsp baking powder

For the topping:
8 green asparagus
2 courgettes|zucchinis, finely chopped
200 g | 7 oz mozzarella, sliced
2 tbsp natural yoghurt
1 tbsp basil leaves, chopped

To garnish:
basil

Nutritional information:
kcal: 448.6
fat: 18.2 g
saturated fat: 6.7 g

Method:
Heat the oven to 200°C (180°C in a fan oven) 400°F, gas 6. Line a cookie sheet with waxed paper.

To make the dough, knead together the cream cheese with 1 tsp salt, olive oil and the egg using an electric hand mixer with dough hooks. Add the flour and baking powder until the mixture forms a smooth dough. Cover and allow to rest for 30 minutes.

Blanch the asparagus for 3 minutes in boiling salted water. Drain and refresh in cold water. Cut into pieces 1/2 cm thick, leave the tips whole.

Roll out the dough on a floured surface to the size of a pizza. Place it on the prepared cookie sheet and form a small crust.

Partbake in the heated oven for 5 minutes.

Arrange the courgette/zucchini and asparagus on the pizza base, season with salt and pepper. Place the mozzarella slices and the asparagus tips on top, drizzle over the yoghurt.

Sprinkle with basil and bake in the hot oven for 20 minutes until golden brown.

Serve garnished with basil leaves.

Monk fish in almond tempura with apple chutney

Prep and cook time: 45 minutes
Cannot be frozen
Serves: 4

Ingredients:

For the apple chutney:

1 tbsp oil
1 tsp mixed oriental spices
1 chilli pepper, very finely chopped
½ tsp turmeric
4 apples, peeled, cores removed, sliced
1 tbsp lemon juice
1 tbsp caster|superfine sugar

For the fish:

100 g | 3 ½ oz | ⅘ cup plain|all purpose flour
1 egg
1 egg yolk
50 g | 1 ¾ oz | ½ cup flaked|slivered almonds
600 g | 21 oz prepared monk fish fillet, cut into 12 equal pieces
oil for deep frying

To garnish:

lime slices

Nutritional information:

kcal: 446.4
fat: 20 g
saturated fat: 3.9 g

Method:

Heat 1 tbsp oil in a pot. Add the spices, chilli and turmeric and fry gently for 30 seconds.

Add the apple slices and fry gently for a few minutes. Add 3 tbsp water, the lemon juice and sugar and simmer for 20 minutes on a low heat, stirring occasionally until the chutney thickens. Cool.

Mix the flour, egg, egg yolk, 200 ml / 7fl oz / 1 cup water and some salt and ground black pepper to form a smooth dough. Allow to rest for 15 minutes and then add the flaked/slivered almonds.

Meanwhile heat enough oil for deep frying in a deep fat fryer or a heavy bottomed saucepan.

Season the fish with salt and ground black pepper and dunk into the almond tempura dough one after the other. Fry in hot oil for 3–4 minutes until golden brown. Pat dry with kitchen paper.

Arrange the fish on plates and serve with the apple chutney.

Baked vegetable rolls with rosemary

Prep and cook time: 25 minutes Bake: 25 minutes
Cannot be frozen
Serves: 4

Ingredients:
500 g | 18 oz | 5/8 cup low -fat cream cheese
3 egg yolks
1 tbsp wine vinegar
1 tsp fresh rosemary, chopped
25 g | 1 oz | 1/4 cup capers, chopped
80 g | 3 oz | 2/3 cup sun-dried tomatoes, in oil, drained and finely chopped
2 courgettes|zucchinis, cut lengthways into thin slices
2 small aubergines|eggplants, cut lengthways into thin slices

To garnish:
5 sprigs of fresh rosemary

Nutritional information:
kcal: 216.3
fat: 7.6 g
saturated fat: 2.6 g

Method:
Heat the oven to 200°C (180°C fan) 400°F, gas 6.

Mix the cream cheese with the egg yolks, vinegar, rosemary, capers and tomatoes and season with salt and ground black pepper.

Spread the cheese mixture on the courgette/zucchini and aubergine/eggplant slices and roll up. Place the rolls in an oven-proof dish greased with a little oil from the tomatoes.

Bake in the preheated oven for 20–25 minutes.
Serve garnished with rosemary.

Turkey breast with yoghurt dip and vegetable rice

Prep and cook time: 40 minutes
Cannot be frozen
Serves: 4

Ingredients:
1 tbsp honey
2 tbsp lime juice
1 chilli pepper, halved, seeds removed and finely chopped
1 tbsp olive oil
650 g | 23 oz turkey breast, cut into four equal slices

For the vegetable rice:
2 garlic cloves, finely chopped
1 tbsp olive oil
1 courgette|zucchini, finely grated
1 carrot, finely grated
1 yellow bell pepper, halved, seeds removed and finely chopped
200 g | 7 oz | 1 cup rice, uncooked
400 ml | 14 fl oz | 1 2/3 cups vegetable stock
2 spring onions|scallions, cut into rings
Cayenne pepper

For the dip:
100 g | 3 1/2 oz | 2/5 cup yoghurt
2 tbsp lemon juice
4 tbsp cress
40 g | 1 1/2 oz bean sprouts

Nutritional information:
kcal: 494.9
fat: 11.8 g
saturated fat: 3.2 g

Method:
Heat the oven to 180°C (160°C fan) 350°F, gas 4.

Mix the honey with the lime juice, chilli pepper and olive oil. Season with salt and then brush the turkey breast with the mixture.

Roast in the oven for 15 minutes. If necessary turn the grill on as well for the last few minutes, to brown turkey.

To make the rice, fry the garlic in 1 tbsp oil. Add the courgette/zucchini, carrot, bell pepper and the rice and fry together lightly.

Add the vegetable stock and let simmer for 10 minutes with a lid on.

Add the spring onions/scallions and cook for a further 10 minutes, until the rice is tender and the liquid is absorbed. Season with salt and Cayenne pepper.

To make the dip, mix the yoghurt with the lemon juice and the cress. Season with salt and ground black pepper.

Remove the turkey slices from the oven, cut diagonally into pieces and serve with the rice and the dip.

Aubergines in garlic sauce

Prep and cook time: 30 minutes
Cannot be frozen
Serves: 4

Ingredients:
3 aubergines|eggplants, cut into 1.5 cm thick slices
1 tbsp olive oil

For the marinade:
2 tbsp olive oil
2 tbsp white wine vinegar
1 small onion, finely chopped
2 garlic clove, finely chopped
1 red chilli pepper, seeds removed, cut into thin strips
1 tbsp fresh parsley, chopped

For the sauce:
200 g | 7 oz | 4/5 cup natural yoghurt
3 garlic cloves, crushed
1 tbsp fresh parsley, chopped

To garnish:
large parsley sprig

Nutritional information:
kcal: 132.6
fat: 8.5 g
saturated fat: 1.6 g

Method:
Arrange the aubergine/eggplant on a large grill pan. Brush with oil and cook under a preheated grill for 10 minutes, turning as needed.

To make the marinade, mix the oil, vinegar, onion, garlic, chilli and parsley, and then season with salt and ground black pepper.

To make the garlic sauce, mix the yoghurt with the garlic and parsley and season with salt and ground black pepper.

Arrange the aubergine/eggplant slices on plates, drizzle with the marinade and serve with the garlic sauce.

Shrimp cakes with sweet chilli dip

Prep and cook time: 20 minutes
Cannot be frozen
Serves: 4

Ingredients:
For the dip:
1/2 red pepper, seeds removed; diced
1 clove garlic, minced
2 fresh red chillies, seeds removed; diced
3 tbsp red wine vinegar
2 tbsp lime juice
1 tbsp sugar

For the shrimp cakes:
500 g | 18 oz prawns|shrimps, chopped
1 egg yolk
1 tbsp cornflour|cornstarch
2 tbsp fish sauce
1 tsp sugar
1 tsp black sesame seeds
8 stalks lemon grass (or wooden skewers)

Nutritional information:
kcal: 204
fat: 4.6 g
saturated fat: 0.9 g

Method:
Put the red pepper, garlic and chillies into a small pan and add approximately 175ml / 6fl oz / 3/4 cup water, the red wine vinegar, lime juice and sugar. Bring to a boil and simmer gently without a lid for about 15 minutes to make the dipping sauce.

Put the prawns/shrimps into a bowl. Mix with the egg yolk, cornflour/cornstarch, fish sauce, sugar, sesame seeds and ground black pepper.

Divide the shrimp mixture into 8 portions and shape into chunky fingers around the lemon grass or wooden skewers.

Grill or fry at a medium heat until golden brown.
Serve with the dipping sauce.

Salsa cruda

Prep and cook time: 15 minutes Steep: 15 minutes
Cannot be frozen
Serves: 4

Ingredients:

- 12 tomatoes, seeds removed and finely chopped
- 50 g | 1 3/4 oz | 1/2 cup sun-dried tomatoes, finely chopped
- 4 spring onions | scallions, finely chopped
- 1 green chilli pepper, halved, seeds removed and finely chopped
- 2 garlic cloves, finely chopped
- 3 tbsp olive oil
- 1 tsp lemon juice
- pinch sugar
- pinch Cayenne pepper
- 4 tbsp basil, chopped

To garnish:

- 1 tbsp spring onions | scallions, finely sliced

Nutritional information:

- kcal: 182.9
- fat: 13.3 g
- saturated fat: 1.6 g

Method:

Mix the tomatoes, sun-dried tomatoes, spring onions/scallions, chilli pepper and the garlic with the olive oil.

Season with lemon juice, sugar, salt, Cayenne pepper and stir in the basil.

Leave for 15 minutes, for the flavours to mingle.

Sprinkle over the spring onions/scallions to garnish and serve with sliced French bread.

Cream cheese dip

Prep and cook time: 20 minutes
Cannot be frozen
Serves: 4

Ingredients:
200 g | 7 oz baguette, sliced
400 g low-fat cream cheese
100 g | 3 ½ oz low-fat natural yoghurt
1 tbsp lemon juice
few drops of Tabasco
2 tomatoes, quartered, seeds removed and finely chopped
4 spring onions|scallions, sliced
2 tbsp chives

Nutritional information:
kcal: 242.7
fat: 3.6 g
saturated fat: 1.8 g

Method:

Toast the baguette until golden-brown.

Mix the cream cheese with the yoghurt and the lemon juice until it forms a smooth paste. Season with salt, ground black pepper and Tabasco.

Keep a handful of tomato and spring onions/scallions aside for the garnish. Mix the rest of them in with the cream cheese. Divide into small bowls.

Garnish with the rest of the tomato, spring onions/scallions and chives and serve with the toasted baguette.

Bulgarian aubergine dip

Prep and cook time: 20 minutes
Cannot be frozen
Serves: 4

Ingredients:
2 aubergines|eggplants, whole
1 small onion, roughly chopped
4 cloves garlic
2 tsp parsley
2 sprigs mint
4 tbsp olive oil
lemon juice

To garnish:
mint sprigs
pinch paprika

Nutritional information:
kcal: 143.05
fat: 10.5 g
saturated fat: 1.2 g

Method:
Heat the oven to 200°C (180°C fan) 400°F, gas 6.

Pierce the aubergines/eggplants with a fork and bake in the oven for 20 minutes until the skin blisters and wrinkles and the flesh feels soft.

Let cool, peel and then remove the stem. Roughly cut the flesh and then put into a blender.

Add the onion, garlic, parsley and mint and 4 tbsp olive oil.

Blend eveything together to make a smooth puree.

Season with lemon juice, salt and ground black pepper, then cover and let cool.

Before serving mix thoroughly once again. Garnish with mint leaves and serve sprinkled with paprika.

Vegetable sticks with a herb dip

Prep and cook time: 25 minutes
Cannot be frozen
Serves: 4

Ingredients:

250 g | 9 oz | 1 cup low-fat cream cheese
100 g | 3 1/2 oz | 2/5 cup natural yoghurt
2 tbsp chopped fresh herbs, e.g. dill, chives, parsley
2 carrots, cut into sticks
2 yellow bell peppers, cut into sticks
2 red bell peppers, cut into sticks
2 sticks celery, cut into smaller sticks
1 cucumber, cut into sticks

To garnish:

1 sprig each of dill and parsley lettuce leaves

Nutritional information:

kcal: 167.3
fat: 3.6 g
saturated fat: 1.7 g

Method:

To make the dip, mix the cream cheese with the yoghurt and herbs then season with salt and ground black pepper. Spoon into a serving bowl.

Arrange the vegetable sticks in another bowl.

Garnish the dip with the dill and parsley and serve with lettuce.

Hummus

Prep and cook time: 15 minutes
Cannot be frozen
Serves: 4

Ingredients:
350 g | 12 oz | 1 3/4 cups chickpeas|garbanzo beans, drained weight from a can
3 cloves garlic, chopped
150 g | 5 oz tahini paste
2 lemons, juice
1/4 tsp cumin
1 tbsp olive oil
1 tsp sweet paprika
4 wholemeal pitta breads, toasted

Make your own tahini:
100 g | 3/4 cup roasted sesame seeds
3 tbsp lemon juice
1 clove garlic, chopped
1 tbsp olive oil

Nutritional information:
kcal: 554.6
fat: 29.7 g
saturated fat: 4.3 g

Method:
Rinse the chickpeas/garbanzo beans under cold running water and put into a processor or blender.

Puree until smooth.

Add the garlic, tahini paste, lemon juice, and cumin. Season with salt and ground black pepper.

Serve drizzled with olive oil and sprinkled with paprika.

Serve with toasted pitta bread.

Make your own tahini:
To make your own tahini, puree all the ingredients together and add as much water as necessary to create a creamy, even paste.

desserts.

Chocolate raspberry roulade

Prep and cook time: 40 minutes Chilling: 3 hours
Can be frozen
Serves: 12

Ingredients:
For the sponge:
4 eggs, separated
100 g | 3 1/2 oz caster|superfine sugar
1 tbsp grated lemon zest
100 g | 3 1/2 oz plain|all purpose flour
20 g | 3/4 oz cocoa powder, 70% cocoa

For the filling:
500 g | 18 oz Greek yoghurt, 0.1% fat
2 tbsp caster|superfine sugar
2 tbsp cocoa powder, 70% cocoa
300 g | 11 oz raspberries, frozen
2 tbsp icing|confectioners' sugar, for dusting

Nutritional information:
kcal: 140.4
fat: 5.07 g
saturated fat: 2.3 g

Method:
Heat the oven to 180°C (160°C fan) 350°F, gas 4. Grease and line a 30 cm x 20 cm (12" x 8") swiss roll tin with non stick paper.

Whisk the egg yolks with the sugar and lemon zest for 5 minutes until thick and foamy.

Sieve the flour and cocoa over the egg yolk mixture and fold in.

Whisk the egg whites until stiffly peaking then fold into the chocolate mixture.

Spread the mixture evenly into the prepared tin.

Bake for about 10 minutes until risen and shrinking from the sides of a tin.

Sprinkle a sheet of non stick paper with 2 tbsp sugar. Turn the sponge out on to this prepared paper and peel off the paper. Cover with a clean damp tea towel and leave to cool completely.

For the filling mix the yoghurt, sugar and cocoa powder.

Spread the chocolate yoghurt over the chocolate sponge and sprinkle over the raspberries.

Lift the paper underneath the chocolate sponge and roll up.

Place on a serving plate with the join side down. Chill until serving.

Dust with icing/confectioners' sugar before serving.

Pear and ginger sorbet

Prep and cook time: 35 minutes Freeze: 4 hours
Can be frozen
Serves: 4

Ingredients:
2 untreated lemons, grated zest and juice
1 tsp fresh root ginger, grated
2 tbsp fructose
2 ripe pears, stones removed, cut into equal pieces
10 g | 1/4 oz | 2/5 cup dark chocolate, grated

To garnish:
1 lemon, zest grated and cut into wedges

Nutritional information:
kcal: 132.5
fat: 1.5 g
saturated fat: 0.6 g

Method:
Put the lemon zest into a pan with the ginger, fructose and 225 ml / 8 floz / 1 cup water. Bring to the boil, then simmer on a low heat for 10 minutes.

Place the pears into another pot with 2 tbsp lemon juice and 4 tbsp water. Cover and poach the pears in it for 8 minutes.

Strain the ginger syrup. Mash the pears and stir into the syrup. Pour into a metal bowl and freeze for 3-4 hours stirring every 30 minutes with a fork so that the sorbet forms small crystals.

To serve, fill the sorbet into high glasses. Sprinkle the grated lemon zest and the chocolate over the top and garnish with the lemon slices.

Meringue pavlova with fresh berries

Prep and cook time: 45 minutes
Cannot be frozen
Serves: 12

Ingredients:
5 egg whites
300 g | 11 oz | 1 ½ cups caster|superfine sugar
1 tsp vinegar
1 tsp vanilla extract
2 tsp cornflour|cornstarch
3 - 4 tbsp flaked|slivered almonds
200 ml | 7 fl oz | ⅞ cup Greek yoghurt, low-fat
500 g | 18 oz | 4 cups mixed berries (strawberries, blackberries, raspberries)
2 tbsp icing|confectioners' sugar

Nutritional information:
kcal: 163.7
fat: 2.8 g
saturated fat: 1.1 g

Method:

Heat the oven to 150°C (140°C fan) 300°F, gas 2.

Beat the egg whites until stiff using a mixer on the highest setting.

Gradually add the sugar. Reduce the speed and gradually add the vinegar, vanilla extract and cornflour/cornstarch.

Line a baking sheet with non-stick baking paper.

Spoon the meringue mixture onto the prepared tray and form into a circle 28 cm / 11" diameter with a depression in the middle.

Sprinkle the almonds over the sides and bake for 45 minutes.

Allow to cool completely.

Transfer the meringue pavlova onto a serving dish.

Spoon in the Greek yoghurt.

Pile the berries on top and serve dusted with icing/confectioners' sugar.

Apple trifle

Prep and cook time: 15 minutes
Cannot be frozen
Serves: 4

Ingredients:
2 sweet apples, cored and diced
4 tbsp apple juice
1 dash lemon juice
100 g | 1 cup low-fat chocolate cookies
1 tsp cocoa powder
250 g | 1 cup natural yoghurt
1 tsp vanilla extract
2 tbsp caster|superfine sugar
cocoa powder, for dusting

Nutritional information:
kcal: 197.7
fat: 2.7 g
saturated fat: 0.9 g

Method:

Put the diced apple into a pan with the apple juice and lemon juice, cover and simmer over a low heat for 2-3 minutes, or until soft. Leave to cool.

Put the biscuits and cocoa powder into a freezer bag and crush roughly.

Mix the yoghurt together with the vanilla extract and sugar.

Fill 4 tall glasses with alternate layers of biscuit crumbs, apple and yoghurt, finishing with yoghurt.

Dust with cocoa powder before serving.

Pancakes with figs and maple syrup

Prep and cook time: 30 minutes
Cannot be frozen
Serves: 4

Ingredients:
200 g | 7 oz | 1 $^{3}/_{5}$ cups plain|all purpose flour
1 pinch salt
2 eggs, separated
3 tbsp olive oil spread
150 g | 5 oz | 9$^{1}/_{2}$ tbsp buttermilk
3 tbsp caster|superfine sugar
3 figs, finely sliced
1 tbsp icing|confectioners' sugar
4 tbsp maple syrup
4-5 figs, cut into slices

To garnish:
4 mint leaves

Nutritional information:
kcal: 369.8
fat: 14.06 g
saturated fat: 3.8 g

Method:
Heat the oven to 110°C (90°C fan) 225°F, gas 4.

Mix the flour with a pinch of salt.

Whisk the egg whites until they form stiff peaks.

Thoroughly mix 2 tbsp olive oil spread with the buttermilk, egg yolks and sugar using an electric whisk. Stir in the flour mixture.

Fold in the egg whites.

Heat the remaining olive oil spread in a large non-stick skillet. Add 5 or 6 fig slices and pour a tbsp of the dough over the top. Turn the heat down to a medium temperature and fry the pancakes on both sides until golden brown.

Lay some more fig slices on top, turn and fry until the surface is golden yellow and slightly crispy.

Place the finished pancakes on a plate in the oven and continue until the dough and the fig slices are used up.

Arrange the pancakes in towers on 4 plates and dust with icing/confectioners' sugar. Drizzle with maple syrup and garnish with mint.

Poached pears with ginger syrup

Prep and cook time: 20 minutes
Cannot be frozen
Serves: 4

Ingredients:
4 ripe pears, peeled leaving stem intact
2 limes, juiced
2 tbsp honey
1 pinch saffron powder
2 tsp root ginger root, grated
200 ml | 7 fl oz | 4/5 cups sweet white wine

Nutritional information:
kcal: 152
fat: 0.6 g
saturated fat: 0.0

Method:
Drizzle the peeled pears immediately with lime juice so they don't discolour.

In a medium saucepan or skillet, dissolve honey in 2tbsp water. Add the saffron and ginger and simmer for 1-2 minutes on a low heat. Add the wine and the pears, cover and simmer for approximately 10 minutes or until the pears are soft but not falling apart. Baste the pears occasionally while they are simmering.

Remove the pears from the pan or skillet and let them cool.

Reduce syrup to about half, strain and let cool.

Serve the pears drizzled with syrup

Pancakes with summer fruits

Prep and cook time: 20 minutes
Cannot be frozen
Serves: 4

Ingredients:
200 g | 7 oz | 1 $^{1}/_{2}$ cups raspberries
1 tsp lemon juice
2 tbsp icing sugar
150 g | 5 oz | 1 $^{1}/_{4}$ cups flour
100 ml | 3 1/2 fl oz | $^{2}/_{5}$ cups semi-skimmed milk
2 eggs
8 tsp vegetable oil
400 g | 14 oz | 3 cups fresh, mixed berries (blackberries, raspberries, blueberries)

Nutritional information:
kcal: 244.6
fat: 4.9 g
saturated fat: 1.3 g

Method:
Puree the 200 g raspberries with a splash of water. Add the lemon juice and icing sugar.

To make the pancakes, put the flour and milk, eggs and add 150 ml | 5fl oz | $^{2}/_{3}$ cup water in a processor and whizz together until smooth (alternatively, put the dry ingredients into the bowl and gradually whisk in the egg, milk and water).

Heat the oil in a non-stick pan. Add a ladleful of the mixture, tilt the pan to cover the base. Cook for 2 minutes, then flip over and cook for 2 more minutes.

Repeat with the remaining pancake mixture, interleaving the pancakes with non-stick paper and keep warm.

Fill the pancakes with berries, fold and serve drizzled with raspberry sauce.

Blueberry yoghurt jelly

Prep and cook time: 25 minutes Chilling: 3 hours
Cannot be frozen
Serves: 4

Ingredients:
10 gelatine sheets
500 g | 18 oz | 2 cups yoghurt, 0.5% fat
50 g | 2 oz | 1/4 cup sugar
1 lemon, juiced
200 g | 7 oz 1 2/5 cups blueberries, selected
1 tbsp orange liquor
200 ml | 7 fl oz | 4/5 cups cream, 30% fat, whipped

Nutritional information:
kcal: 293.8
fat: 15.5 g
saturated fat: 9.2 g

Method:
Soften the gelatine in water.

Put the yoghurt, sugar and lemon juice into a blender with the blueberries.

Whiz together to a smooth puree.

Squeeze out the gelatine and heat in a small pot with the orange liquor until dissolved.

Mix in with the yoghurt mixture and stir in the cream.

Pour into 4 moulds and chill for at least 3 hours.

Upturn the moulds and serve garnished with mint leaves.

Peach and yoghurt trifle with raspberries

Prep and cook time: 25 minutes
Cannot be frozen
Serves: 4

Ingredients:

2 tbsp runny honey
400 g | 14 oz | 1 1/2 cups natural yoghurt, low-fat
2 white peaches, stones removed, sliced
8 lady fingers (sponge fingers), roughly broken
4 tbsp dessert wine or sherry
100 g | 3 1/2 oz | 3/4 cup raspberries
1 tbsp flaked|slivered almonds, toasted

Nutritional information:

kcal: 207.2
fat: 5.3 g
saturated fat: 1.5 g

Method:

Mix the honey with the yoghurt.

Put a spoonful of the yoghurt mix into the base of 4 glass dishes.

Arrange some peach slices on top.

Place some sponge fingers on top and drizzle over the dessert wine or sherry.

Spoon over the rest of the yoghurt mix.

Top with the rest of the peach slices.

Finish with the raspberries and the toasted, flaked/slivered almonds.

Berry granita

Prep and cook time: 15 minutes Freezing: 4 hours
Can be frozen
Serves: 4

Ingredients:
150 g | 5 oz caster|superfine sugar
500 g | 18 oz frozen berries (strawberries, raspberries, blueberries and blackberries)
1/2 lemon, juiced

To garnish:
4 mint leaves

Nutritional information:
kcal: 214.3
fat: 0.79 g
saturated fat: 0.06 g

Method:
Put the sugar into a pan with 200ml water. Bring to the boil and simmer for 5 minutes.

Put the frozen berries into a blender with the sugar syrup and lemon juice.

Blend until smooth.

Mix well, transfer to a freezer-proof container and freeze (or put into an ice cream machine).

Freeze for 4 hours, stirring well every hour (or blend in an ice cream machine).

Spoon the berry granita into glasses.

Garnish with mint leaves.

Quark cake with apricot filling

Prep and cook time: 1 hour 20 minutes
Can be frozen
Serves: 12

Ingredients:

1 kg | 35 oz | 4 1/8 cups low-fat quark
250 g | 9 oz | 1 cup low-fat cream cheese
3 eggs
200 g | 7 oz | 7/8 cup caster|superfine sugar
2 tbsp vanilla extract
3 tbsp cornflour|cornstarch
1 tsp baking powder
50 g | 1 3/4 oz | 5 cups semolina|cream of wheat
850 g | 30 oz | 4 cups canned apricots, drained

Nutritional information:
kcal: 248.8
fat: 2.1 g
saturated fat: 0.7 g

Method:

Heat the oven to 180°C (160°C fan) 350°F, gas 4. Grease and line a 23cm 9" spring form tin.

Put the quark, cream cheese, and eggs into a mixing bowl and mix well.

Add the sugar, vanilla extract, cornflour/cornstarch, baking powder and semolina/cream of wheat to the bowl.

Mix all the ingredients together.

Put half of the quark mixture into the prepared springform pan, add the apricots in a layer and cover with the rest of the mixture.

Bake for 1 hour until firm.

Chill and slice into wedges to serve.

Apple compote with vanilla yoghurt and toasted rolled oats

Prep and cook time: 20 minutes
Cannot be frozen
Serves: 4

Ingredients:
4 cooking apples, quartered cored and chopped
1 lemon, juice
4 tbsp brown sugar
1 vanilla pod, cut in half
4 tbsp rolled oats
1 tbsp low-fat spread
200 g | 7 oz | 3/4 cup low-fat yoghurt
1 tsp vanilla extract

Nutritional information:
kcal: 198.1
fat: 1.7 g
saturated fat: 0.3 g

Method:

Put the apples into a pan with the lemon juice, 2 tbsp sugar and the vanilla pod, cover and bring to the boil, then simmer for 5 minutes until the apples are tender.

Meanwhile put the rolled oats into a pan with 1 tbsp sugar and the low-fat olive oil spread. Heat and stir for a few minutes until the oats turn golden. Remove from the heat and leave to cool.

Mix together the yoghurt with 1 tbsp sugar and the vanilla extract.

Spoon the apple compote into glasses, add a layer of vanilla yoghurt and serve sprinkled with golden oats.

Panna cotta with nectarines

Prep and cook time: 25 minutes Chill: 4 hours
Cannot be frozen
Serves: 4

Ingredients:
500 ml | 18 fl oz | 2 cups cream
3 tbsp sugar
1 vanilla pod, cut in half lengthways, seeds scraped out
6 sheets gelatine

To garnish:
2 nectarines, sliced
4 sprigs mint

Nutritional information:
kcal: 225.2
fat: 12.6 g
saturated fat: 7.6 g

Method:

Put the cream, sugar, vanilla seeds and the pod into a pan and bring to the boil. Remove from the heat.

Soften the gelatine in cold water. Squeeze out well and add to the hot vanilla cream. Dissolve, stirring continuously.

Cool stirring occasionally until the cream begins to gel.

Remove the vanilla pod, rinse 4 small moulds in cold water and fill with the vanilla cream.

Chill for at least 3 hours.

Upturn the panna cotta from the moulds onto dessert plates. Serve garnished with the nectarines and the mint.

Peach compote with yoghurt, saffron and mint

Prep and cook time: 20 minutes Chilling: 30 minutes
Cannot be frozen
Serves: 4

Ingredients:

1 untreated lemon, juiced and zest finely grated

150 ml | 5 fl oz | 5/8 cup sweet vermouth, or port

3 tbsp sugar

1 pinch saffron threads

4 ripe peaches, halved and stones removed

to serve:

4 tbsp natural yoghurt, low-fat

1 tbsp chopped, fresh mint

mint leaves, to garnish

Nutritional information:

kcal: 121.08

fat: 0.3 g

saturated fat: 0.1 g

Method:

Put the lemon zest and juice into a pan and begin to heat.

Add the vermouth or port, the sugar and saffron and 225 ml / 8fl oz/ 1 cup of water.

Add the peaches and bring to the boil.

Turn off the heat, cover and allow to steep.

To serve, mix together the yoghurt and chopped mint.

In bowls, serve the peaches drizzled with the sauce the mint yoghurt.

Garnish with mint leaves.

Champagne berry jelly

Prep and cook time: 30 minutes Chilling: 4 hours
Cannot be frozen
Serves: 10-12 (1 bundt mould)

Ingredients:
10 gelatine sheets
100 g | 3 1/2 oz | 1/2 cup caster|superfine sugar
1 untreated lemon, finely grated zest
3 tbsp framboise (raspberry liqueur)
1 kg | 35 oz mixed berries (strawberries, blueberries, raspberries, blackberries)
1 bottle champagne, 700 ml

To garnish:
100 g | 3 1/2 oz mixed berries
mint leaves or berry leaves

Nutritional information:
kcal: 121.6
fat: 0.6 g
saturated fat: 0.0 g

Method:

Put the gelatine into a bowl and cover with cold water to soften.

Bring the sugar and the lemon zest to a boil in 100 ml / 4fl oz / 1/2 cup water. Simmer for 10 minutes until it becomes syrup-like in consistency. Take out the zest and remove the syrup from the heat.

Squeeze out the gelatine, warm in the framboise (raspberry liqueur) and dissolve. Add to the syrup and let cool.

Place the berries in a bundt mould (or similar).

Add the champagne to the syrup and pour it over the berries - the fruit should be covered. Cover with cling film and chill for at least 4 hours.

To serve, upturn the jelly/jello out of the mould and garnish with fresh berries and mint or berry leaves.

index

index.

index.